Brand Causality

A step-by-step process for defining your brand's
best positioning and maximising customer engagement

AF807575

Craig Hunter

Brand Causality

Published by Impressum, Newcastle NSW

© Craig Hunter 2021

www.blacksheepgroup.com.au

Cover and internal design by Impressum www.impressum.com.au
National Library of Australia Cataloguing-in-Publication entry

Author: Hunter, Craig

Title: Brand Causality / Craig Hunter

ISBN: 978-1-922588-07-4 (print)
978-1-922588-08-1 (ebook)

All rights reserved. No part of this publication may be reproduced, stored in, or introduced into a retrieval system, or transmitted, in any form, or by any means (electronic, mechanical, photocopying, recording or otherwise) without the prior written permission of the publisher.

NATIONAL LIBRARY OF AUSTRALIA

A catalogue record for this work is available from the National Library of Australia

I would like to thank my mentors: Paul Feldwick for introducing me to the wonderful world of Strategy Planning, Christine Asbury, for teaching me how to do it and Mike Daniels for helping me craft my skills. Professor Francis Farrelly for his guidance on writing this book and all my clients past and present for their support and encouragement. My family: my Mum and sister, my sons, Ollie, Tom and Arch, my wonderful partner, Chrissie, and her son Denis, for their inspiration and support. My editor Gina and publisher Emma at Impressum for their patience and guidance.

CONTENTS

INTRODUCTION:

Small Questions, Big Ideas

Positioning a brand successfully in the marketplace and the mind of the customer is vital to the everyday running and long-term success of a business. Positioning your brand requires a simple, sequential and convergent framework. This is where the Brand Causality Model can be utilised. Drawing on 20 years of practical experience, the Brand Causality Model was developed to guide you to consider and strategically express your brand to engage your consumer. It uses simple, straightforward questions to help you build key truths about your business and inform your brand positioning.

This book is for anyone in business – whether established or just starting out, in a large company or flying solo – who is interested in positively influencing how their customers think and feel about their product or service. It is about strategically positioning your brand in such a way that people will be predisposed to engage with it. This is a complex task, requiring a sequential framework that leads to a brand positioning true to the product, engaging to the customer and distinct from the competition.

The method I present in this guide draws on my extensive experience across market and consumer research, advertising and brand strategy. It has been shaped in the fires of practical experience and includes aspects of contemporary psychology, behavioural, economic and neuromarketing insight, as well as common principles of brand positioning strategy.

In my career, I have worked in advertising, market research and brand consultancies for large multi-national and smaller national companies across the world. In running my own consultancy for the last 10 years, I have gravitated towards brand positioning strategy, usually informed by qualitative and quantitative research. I consider myself very lucky to have had the opportunity to help brand owners define and direct their brands to places that give them satisfaction and pride while also creating salience for their customers. The process is exciting, revealing and inspiring. Through it, I have greatly refined my own brand positioning method, and now I want to share this knowledge and skillset more widely.

In this guide, I reveal the small, straightforward questions that any brand owner or manager can answer. These answers will inform and inspire critical concepts, or truths, for the brand. These truths are the building blocks that help inform the most significant concepts within a brand positioning strategy: The Brand Story and the Brand Essence. The Brand Causality Model is a framework that uses the answers to simple, small questions to inform and define complex, big brand strategy principles. It is, therefore, an exercise in causality, hence the name of my model: The Brand Causality Model.

Causality, in the sense that I am using it, is influenced by one event, process or state (a cause, [questions]), contributes to the production of another event (an effect [answers]), where the cause is partly responsible for the effect, and the effect is partially dependent on the cause. The Brand Causality Model can assist you in developing a strategic 'blueprint' or 'true north' for your brand, which will impact the short-term running and long-term success of your business.

The majority of the questions and concepts contained within this guide are, in isolation, not new or original. Still, the overall process of brand causality (to the best of my knowledge) is original. The difference between great and good lies in the details of the techniques, approaches and direction in the following pages.

Before giving you an overview of my model and how I will break it down for you in this guide, it's helpful to look at where my approach sits in the wider conversation around brand positioning.

A Practical Brand Positioning Guide

The practice of brand strategy, specifically the theory or frameworks for brand definition or positioning, was created, or at least defined, by Ries and Trout (1981) who published *Positioning: A Battle for Your Mind.* The term was first used in a 1969 article in *Advertising Age.* In the 1990s, brand strategy was focused more on the definition or transformation of brands within a challenger context. Jean-Marie Dru's *Disruption* (1996) and Adam Morgan's *Eating the Big Fish* (1999) provided challenger brand definition frameworks by the advertising industry's best thinkers. There are many similar frameworks utilising aspects of this initial theory in existence today, such as brand positioning approaches created by digital, advertising, media, brand and marketing agencies, as well as models created and utilised by the larger brand owners themselves.

The focus given to brand positioning by brand owners and their supporting partners is evidence of its critical role in the brand's success. Considering the importance of successful brand positioning, the lack of guides to achieve it is surprising. The idea of brand positioning has been practised since before the famous Avis 'We try harder' campaign of the 1960s. But guides or 'toolkits' that outline the process required to help position brands are few. Why?

I can offer a few explanations. There are established, fundamental principles in brand positioning, which operate as a guide. Most academic qualifications in marketing or business offer these (as does a quick Google search), but the specific techniques and questions are superficial within these broad academic courses. In brand positioning, the more general, traditional parts are much easier to articulate than the detailed process that results in the answers.

The sometimes mystical art of brand positioning is often bound within the proprietary world of brand service agencies and consultants, who rightly protect their specific approaches (though they are often similar, as any experienced brand owner will tell you). Whatever the cause, the result is the same; a lack of visibility, discussion and necessary debate about the best frameworks or models to position a brand.

In this book, the focus is practical. I quickly establish a model but focus on the process that, through a series of sequential questions, will help you arrive at a meaningful brand positioning. It is, in many ways, the reverse of much existing literature, in that it informs on principles through questions and techniques that help us arrive at the right answers.

Over the years, I have been exposed to many international advertising, branding and media agency techniques to 'define' or 'transform' brands. Each may be different, with different journeys and areas of focus, but they invariably lead to the same fundamental questions: 'What does your brand do?' 'Why is it different?' and 'What are its vision and values?' On the face of it, these are quite simple questions. Still, looking at them right now, would you be able to confidently answer them? Or could you be sure your key stakeholders (other management, employees or agency partners) would be able to answer them consistently? More importantly, are you sure your answers are the best they can be? Positioning a brand by using responses to these fundamental questions is difficult and, to my mind, dangerous. They are also a little dated and generic.

In contrast, the Brand Causality Model is a guide to positioning a brand in the marketplace and in the mind of the consumer through the use of simple, straightforward questions to help build key truths about the business to inform the brand positioning. Brand positioning is the common foundation for the development of a brand and business.

Good strategic thinking, whether done in isolation or within a workshop context, needs a sequential framework, a set of simple guiding questions that force convergent (rather than divergent) thinking, defined and communicated with simple, concise concepts.

The set of questions in this guide are ones that I have changed, refined and examined from different points of view over the past 15 years. I believe the strength in my approach is in its simplicity. The Brand Causality method forces the individual or team into a 'strategic funnel', from which there are only limited endpoints. It then utilises those endpoints to inform the Brand Story. The Brand Story inspires one single-minded idea that encapsulates the brand and defines what it is: what we call the Brand Essence.

Let's take a closer look at the model.

The Brand Causality Model

In chapter one, we will take a deep dive into the method that lies behind the Brand Causality Model. Here, you can just dip your toe in to get a sense for where we are headed.

Defining the Brand Story and Brand Essence is not an exercise in high-order strategy. It is, however, essential to the everyday running and long-term success of a business. The successful definition of the Brand Story and subsequent Brand Essence requires a convergent process that gently yet methodically guides us to a solution. It is a solution based on the fundamentals of the business; I call these fundamentals 'Core Concepts'.

These Core Concepts are, in their own right, powerful statements. We live in a world of time scarcity, information overload, complex management structures and ever-increasing marketing services. It is challenging to build a shared understanding of the brand internally and externally. The power in the Core Concepts is not just in definition but shared understanding: simple statements that clearly define 'what business we are in', 'what we are trying to achieve for our customer' and 'our cultural and consumer social guidelines'. There is incredible potential and power for an organisation that knows (and lives) these statements from the boardroom to the coalface of customer interaction and experience.

The Core Concepts are crucial. They can, therefore, not be arrived at without guidance or detailed knowledge of the business. The Core Concepts need to be based on what we call 'Formative Questions'; formative in the sense that they provide the basis to arrive at the Core Concept. The nature of the Formative Question is also influenced by the Core Concept we are seeking.

The Formative Questions guide the individual or group in defining the Core Concepts. These questions are by no means esoteric or creative – the most rational mind could successfully answer them. There is no magic formula at work here, just an exercise in consequential thinking. With the guide we also give plenty of guidance and examples as a means to illustrate how to answer the questions. When summarising complex ideas, language, expression and style become critical.

The first Core Concept, the Brand's Business (which we will unpack further in chapter 2), is about just that, the 'business'. The Formative Questions here focus on history, heritage and development of the business and bring us to current day challenges. We are ultimately looking to define the brand's core business and its speciality or focus.

The second Core Concept, the Brand's Truth (chapter 3), is about the consumer. The Formative Questions here seek to identify our category and determine the consumer goals within. We then match our brand assets and strengths to a key goal, ultimately defining how we help the consumer within our category achieve their desired goal.

The third Core Concept, the Brand's Spirit (chapter 4), is about the brand's beliefs, purpose and character. The Formative Questions seek, first, to identify the key positive brand beliefs, second, to set a broader consumer purpose for the brand, and third, to define the aspects required to fulfil its purpose.

Once these Core Concepts have been articulated, they are used to develop the next stage in the process, the Defining Concepts (chapter 5). The first of these is the Brand Story. The use of stories in branding is well documented. The human tradition to encapsulate the brand within a story makes it more accessible, human and memorable, hence more successful. The Core Concepts have been developed to articulate your Brand's Business, Truth and Spirit. They comfortably come together to form a story, which we limit to 100 words to ensure it doesn't become a catch-all novel!

With the Brand Story written, you now reach the end of the process, the creation of the Brand Essence. Any discipline that uses few words to describe broad concepts requires a degree of creativity, as well as the ability to 'hold' everything you know about your brand and synthesise it into one powerful idea – the Brand Essence. The process articulated through the Brand Causality Model makes that 'holding' simpler, in that each answer is a natural convergence of those before it. Hence, we will be led by the Brand Story in finding the Brand Essence.

The Brand Causality Model

FORMATIVE QUESTIONS	CORE CONCEPTS	DEFINING CONCEPTS
Our Heritage: Why was this brand created? Our Challenge: What is the key barrier to growth and profitability?	THE BRAND'S BUSINESS: The core business and its speciality or focus	The Brand Story: The confluence of the core concepts in a story The Brand Essence: A simple, familiar, emotionally engaging idea
Consumer Goal: What are the consumer goals within category? Brand Assets: What are the brand's strengths?	THE BRAND'S TRUTH: How we help the consumer achieve their goal	
Belief System: What cultural beliefs drive the brand? Brand Feeling: What are the brand's purpose and character?	THE BRAND'S SPIRIT: The cultural and consumer social guidelines	

The Brand Causality Model is ultimately an exercise in convergent, sequential thinking and concise expression. It begins with the Formative Questions that inform the Core Concepts. After answering the Formative Questions, we will work through each of the Core Concepts in turn, starting with the Brand's Business, then the Brand's Truth and then the Brand's Spirit. When we have completed all three Core Concepts, we will be able to articulate the Defining Concepts. The Defining Concepts include the longer Brand Story, which, in turn, inspires the shorter Brand Essence: a simple, familiar, emotionally engaging, all-encompassing idea that defines and directs the brand's future.

Let's get started.

1

The Brand Causality Method

When I am setting out on a long travel journey, I find it most motivating to have a clear picture of my destination firmly in mind. Therefore, before heading into a detailed, step-by-step guide though the Brand Causality Model's constituent parts, I invite you to first look broadly at the whole method and its outcomes.

Within this guide, I have used fictitious yet familiar illustrative examples. For this chapter, I have used two typical bank brands – a 'national bank' and 'digital bank'. The national bank is a national financial institution and has a ubiquitous high street presence. It offers consumer and business products through its branch, online and mobile services. For our purposes, we will imagine the national bank's focus is more on the consumer and (smaller) business services (and less on high-net-worth individuals or corporations). The second example, the digital bank, is a newer online-only style institution. It offers limited products and services through all digital channels. It is, therefore, able to reduce its fees and charges because of its business model.

Establishing the Brand's Business

<table>
<tr><th>FORMATIVE QUESTIONS</th><th>CORE CONCEPTS</th><th>DEFINING CONCEPTS</th></tr>
<tr><td>Our Heritage: Why was this brand created?
Our Challenge: What is the key barrier to growth and profitability?</td><td>THE BRAND'S BUSINESS: The core business and its speciality or focus</td><td rowspan="3">The Brand Story:
The confluence of the core concepts in a story

The Brand Essence:
A simple, familiar, emotionally engaging idea</td></tr>
<tr><td>Consumer Goal: What are the consumer goals within category?
Brand Assets: What are the brand's strengths?</td><td>THE BRAND'S TRUTH:
How we help the consumer achieve their goal</td></tr>
<tr><td>Belief System: What cultural beliefs drive the brand?
Brand Feeling: What are the brand's purpose and character?</td><td>THE BRAND'S SPIRIT:
The cultural and consumer social guidelines</td></tr>
</table>

We first seek to define what business our brand is in through understanding its past, present and future. The Formative Questions are designed to focus our thinking on the brand's core business focus – what the brand brings to the category. On one level, answering these questions is deceptively easy. However, seeking to define our Brand's Business and core focus is never as easy as it seems. The answer has an enormous impact on our brand and business. Hence, we break down the question into conceptually simple areas.

Formative Question: Our Heritage

Why was this brand created?

The first Formative Question focuses on the past and defining key moments. We consider the heritage of the brand and look for a single historical thought, idea or theme that has been significant in shaping the brand. My favourite Churchill quote explains why: 'The farther backward you can look, the farther forward you can see'. Using our fictitious example of the banking institutions, let's consider the typical national bank brand and new digital-only bank.

- **National Bank:** Established over 100 years ago, we have grown with the nation, supporting the individuals, communities and industry that built it.
- **Digital Bank:** Created without the cumbersome infrastructures and bureaucracy of the traditional big banks, we offer a new, stripped-back banking model.

Formative Question: Our Challenge

What is the key barrier to growth and profitability?

Here we explore the contemporary challenges that all businesses and brands face by exploring the brand's landscape using different methods to identify key barriers to growth. We will look for recurrent themes, threads or origins of the different challenges and try to express them as a single key challenge. We ultimately want to define a single problem (but up to three are acceptable).

- **National Bank:** We are trusted yet lack connection. There is an absence of a simple, engaging and unifying theme across our services with which individuals and businesses can connect.
- **Digital Bank:** We have yet to establish brand trust and longevity assurance. The competitive nature of our products

and services has not been properly communicated. A reason for online-only banking, in an age of instant connection, is not well established.

Core Concept 1: The Brand's Business

The core business and its specialty or focus

With an understanding of the past and current business dynamics, we move to the first Core Concept. Here, considering the past and present, we decide on the future of the brand's category definition. What is the key aspect or definition of the business, and what does it bring to its category? What is the focus or speciality of the business? All of which leads us to a concise definition of the Brand's Business.

- **National Bank:** 'We provide access to a range of financial services across all of our customers' life stages.'
- **Digital Bank:** 'We supply banking essentials at a low cost through all digital platforms.'

The process will force consideration and consensus around the definition of our role in the category, of 'where we want to be' from a business viewpoint. We might redefine our market or even category or business or agree with the current definition. Either way, it is a critical decision and sets the direction for the rest of the process. (We will also discuss expression in the following step-by-step breakdown).

Application

Based on profitability, the business strategy should inform the brand strategy – you can build a powerful brand, but if there's no profit, there's no future! Brand positioning, in turn, gives the business strategy focus and direction. Without which, a business is always more ineffective. There is an obvious benefit from understanding and being aligned to a brand's core focus.

Often, brands will redefine their focus. I have seen brands focus on smaller categories, shedding recent expansion and 'getting back to their roots'. This was demonstrated by Steve Jobs' famous speech to the Apple faithful on returning and focusing on consumer electronics. Might Kodak have survived if it had redefined its Brand's Business beyond conventional photography?

I have also seen brands that are ready to 'stretch their legs' into other categories and redefine their business. Virgin is the best example of a high-profile brand that, through clear business focus, can effortlessly glide into different categories. Finally, and perhaps most commonly, brands often want to define precisely what has made them successful before they lose the focus due to expansion.

Brands live and grow in consumer heads and hearts but are initially created and curated by businesses. A business that understands its brand's role will have a competitive advantage over those that don't. A business that is flexible and progressive in the way it defines and considers its brand's focus will always be well placed to grow share and margin. Unless we are clear and agreed on what the brand does, it is impossible to move from the business to the consumer world.

Establishing the Brand's Truth

<table>
<tr><th>FORMATIVE QUESTIONS</th><th>CORE CONCEPTS</th><th>DEFINING CONCEPTS</th></tr>
<tr><td>Our Heritage: Why was this brand created?
Our Challenge: What is the key barrier to growth and profitability?</td><td>THE BRAND'S BUSINESS: The core business and its speciality or focus</td><td rowspan="3">The Brand Story:
The confluence of the core concepts in a story

The Brand Essence:
A simple, familiar, emotionally engaging idea</td></tr>
<tr><td>Consumer Goal: What are the consumer goals within category?
Brand Assets: What are the brand's strengths?</td><td>THE BRAND'S TRUTH:
How we help the consumer achieve their goal</td></tr>
<tr><td>Belief System: What cultural beliefs drive the brand?
Brand Feeling: What are the brand's purpose and character?</td><td>THE BRAND'S SPIRIT:
The cultural and consumer social guidelines</td></tr>
</table>

With the Brand's Business defined, we can move on to the next Core Concept and consider our consumers' goal within the category. Unifying the consumer goal and our brand assets to create a relevant Brand Truth.

We all have continuously changing needs from those that are basic to those that are complex, dependent on a multitude of internal and external factors. The successful product and service brands within the marketplace meet and satisfy those needs. If a brand can influence the customer so that they associate that brand with their desired need, it is more likely to be favoured.

In today's mature, competitive and complex marketplaces, brands that consider the consumer need or 'goal' are more likely to be relevant and make a connection. For example, we all need water, and most have access through a faucet (tap). Still, for convenience, health, prestige and numerous other factors, we end up spending billions of dollars on bottled water. We can be limited by distribution, but we often, if not always, have a choice. The bottled water brands that answer a specific consumer desire or goal are likely to be favoured and more successful. Identifying precisely what these goals are and understanding the motivation behind them at a category level is critical.

This may seem obvious, and it is! It is also accepted wisdom within many brand positioning models (based on the original assumptions of Ries and Trout) that we should position the brand in the existent reality of the consumer and their needs. However, when it comes to selling, many companies create products or services first (or have historical products and services) before considering how to sell them based on the product or service's attributes and benefits.

Most products and services have evolved to meet a functional need or provide a necessary service. As markets evolve and choice within every category becomes numerous, the ability to differentiate a product or service attribute (e.g., speed) or benefit (e.g., time-saving) diminish. The discipline of brand positioning is continually evolving. The simplistic core belief within this concept is that we must first consider our consumer and align the product or service in a way that will help them reach their goal.

This is a 'consumer-over-product approach', which believes our brand's existence and success in the marketplace is dependent on answering the goal of the consumer in a way that utilises the brand's existent, past or future assets.

Theoretical note

It is relevant to discuss here the concept of the past, present and future concerning this Core Concept and the brand positioning process overall. Some questions guide to the past, others to the present; therefore, follow the guidance where offered. In other questions, there is a choice. Every brand session I have run is different in some way. In some sessions, people are looking to define what is a currently successful brand, others are looking for growth or to break a feeling of stagnation. Others feel the brand is broken, and they need to start afresh. Depending on these needs, we can employ the concept of past, present and future to varying and obvious degrees. Although brand positioning should always be based on an understanding of the past, it must also give clear direction to the future. As we progress through the guide, we will note time-based guidelines.

Formative Question: Consumer Goal

What are the consumer goals within category?

The first Formative Question within this section seeks to define the key consumer goal within category. Here we encourage more comprehensive 'category thinking' than specific 'brand thinking'. We can spend so much of our professional lives thinking about specific brand or product benefits, yet we seldom 'come up for air' and consider the overall purpose and service to the consumer of our category. It is refreshing and enlightening when we do. Categories seldom have one consumer goal, so it's a good idea to develop multiple answers to this question. When satisfied, do not try to converge or select the goal most appropriate to our brand (it will be natural to do so), but move on to the second Formative Question.

- **National Bank:** The category customer wants a bank it can trust, that provides simplicity, familiarity and specialist expertise.
- **Digital Bank:** The category customer wants a new way of banking, with tailored products and seamless delivery.

Formative Question: Brand Assets

What are the brand strengths?

Within this section we focus on the product or service itself. We break out and focus on the brands attributes, and then group the attributes into common themes, expressed as brand benefits.

A *brand attribute* is an actual tangible component of the brand and/or a strength or skill that our brand utilises to create appeal for the customer (e.g., no sugar, 24 hours car servicing). Once those attributes are determined, we progress to the second part of the question to consider our own, not the category, *brand benefits.* A brand benefit is the product or consumer value resulting from the attributes (e.g., healthy, less disruption to life).

In this question, we arrive at the Brand Assets through firstly determining the brand attributes (its product/service attributes and features) then using those attributes to shape our own brand benefits (the product and consumer benefits).

Let's go through the process with our banking examples, first their brand attributes and then the corresponding brand benefits:

- **National Bank brand attributes:** We have multiple branches and ATMs, as well as 24-hours online and mobile banking services. We have multiple products including accounts, mortgages, credit cards and personal loans for consumers and much more for business banking. We have over 100 years' experience in providing financial services. We provide personal bankers when and where you need them.

- **National Bank brand benefits:** We have an easily accessible, extensive product range. With the experience and expertise to advise you when and where you need it.
- **Digital Bank brand attributes:** We provide the banking essentials, with low-cost fees, products are available 24/7, advice across all digital and social platforms.
- **Digital Bank brand benefits:** We are flexible, active and customer orientated. We offer a new and different choice within the market.

Brand positioning strategy requires sacrifice for brevity and clarity. To achieve this, we will see throughout the model techniques as above. In this case we ask ourselves a question (brand attributes), that informs the answer (brand benefits). It is the brand's benefits that become the answer to the overall question of what the brand's assets are.

Core Concept 2: The Brand's Truth

How do we help the consumer achieve their goal?

We now begin the process of convergence – a process of 'matching' the consumer goal and brand assets (the brand's benefits), resulting in the definition of the Brand's Truth. Considering the previous consumer goals and our brand asset benefits, what would be the most motivating consumer goal? And what brand asset benefits fit best?

- **National Bank:** When you need us most in life, we will be there to offer the right advice.

- **Digital Bank:** We provide a new, straightforward and better value approach to banking.

Application

A universal understanding of the Brand's Truth will have a profound and liberating impact on every aspect of our business. The process can be illuminating for businesses, revolutionising and progressing them from manufacturing products or supplying services, to meeting consumer goals – a significant strategic shift in business and brand strategy.

With an increased understanding of the consumer and their goals, there is an immediate impact on current and future products or services. How products and services are presented can be refocused. New development cycles can become more concentrated and directed.

In my experience, better brand teams are focused on fewer things. Understanding brand assets can help businesses move towards doing less, better. They can discard or reprioritise secondary assets and focus on core assets, in line with their business focus (the Brand's Business) and the Brand's Truth.

The Brand's Truth sets businesses and their brands free. It gives direction to business, product/service, brand and communications strategy.

Establishing the Brand's Spirit

FORMATIVE QUESTIONS	CORE CONCEPTS	DEFINING CONCEPTS
Our Heritage: Why was this brand created? Our Challenge: What is the key barrier to growth and profitability?	THE BRAND'S BUSINESS: The core business and its speciality or focus	The Brand Story: The confluence of the core concepts in a story The Brand Essence: A simple, familiar, emotionally engaging idea
Consumer Goal: What are the consumer goals within category? Brand Assets: What are the brand's strengths?	THE BRAND'S TRUTH: How we help the consumer achieve their goal	
Belief System: What cultural beliefs drive the brand? Brand Feeling: What are the brand's purpose and character?	THE BRAND'S SPIRIT: The cultural and consumer social guidelines	

Often 'the last nine yards' in brand positioning strategy, but always in my experience the most important, this is the most crucial Core Concept within modern brand strategy. It is also often the least considered. We are social, empathetic and emotionally led creatures. It should be no surprise that we make decisions emotionally (if not always, at least initially). Accepting this, the 'overall nature' of our brand is critical – how people 'feel' about the brand, what 'impression' they have of the brand, what they 'associate' with the brand. Our brand's driving beliefs, ultimate purpose and its character ultimately shape the perception and feelings towards the brand – the Brand's Spirit.

Understandably, we are much more comfortable (in business) with tangible, objective and rationally led debate. However, this often results in assigning generic platitudes and bumper-sticker phrases to our brand's character. As we understand more about how the brain works and why we make the choices we make, one thing is clear – the feelings and associations, the character of our brand, is critical to the impression it makes and, therefore, impacts propensity to purchase. I believe that the impression we make through the brand's character or spirit, is what endures most over time in the consumers mind (or at least some subconscious emotional attributes endure). There is a wonderful case study that demonstrated that just being exposed to the Apple logo made respondents 20–30% more creative (versus exposure to the IBM logo). This process requires us to understand how our brand fits into the world and define a set of 'social guidelines' for it: a brand universe where 'what we stand for', 'believe in' and 'how we act' defines and differentiates our brand.

More than ever, brands need to understand 'who they are', so they can react to the increasing pace of modern business. This transformation requires a brand and the company behind it, to understand the brand thoroughly. There are often multiple internal and external stakeholders who manage the inputs and outputs of a brand – the board, management team, various departments, suppliers and partners – and they must all be *completely aligned*. The oldest 'cost of entry' for brand management is consistency, but the latest technology makes this more of a challenge than ever! Hence the need for some clear and concise guidelines.

Formative Question: Belief System

What cultural beliefs drive the brand?

The first Formative Question in this section considers the internal culture and its driving beliefs. What beliefs have shaped us over time?

The 'Our Heritage' question is very useful here. Considering our conclusions to date, what beliefs are emergent or fixed?

I prefer to create a brand belief system to more traditional cultural values because it more accurately describes reality. Over the years when working with clients, I have become frustrated with inherited or historical brand values that are meaningless to the people in the company, who are supposed to live them. A belief system is more organic, dynamic and evolving. It demands that we consider the brand's cultural principles as an interconnected system; each element dependent and supporting the other.

Think of a brand as a dynamic organism that has evolved (in part) because of fundamental inner beliefs. What are those inner beliefs? This is always a fascinating question – turning the spotlight inward often has interesting results. Within this section and the broader methodology, we can choose existing beliefs, build on those beliefs, or create new ones.

Considering our 'usual suspect' internal brand values is a helpful frame of reference for this question because they are already known. However, they should only be a starting point. For example, in most brand workshops, the term 'innovative' crops up a lot. It may well be valid, but from an internal cultural point of view, what does it mean? Within every business supporting a brand, there will be core beliefs that work together to form a belief system.

- **National Bank:** We believe in responsibility, understanding and expertise. Beliefs that guide us through the good and bad, boom and bust of our customers' lives and our nation's history.
- **Digital Bank:** We believe in better, an agile and transparent approach. We are a digital innovator forging a new way forward in financial products and services.

Formative Question: Brand Feeling

What are the brand's purpose and character?

Beliefs are deep in nature and learnt over time through experience. In the next Formative Question, we consider the brand feeling. A feeling is 'something that you feel through the mind or through the senses' (Oxford Dictionaries definition). It is a response, an intuitive reaction, much more immediate and emotional.

Within this part of the process, we want to influence how our customer sees and therefore feels about us. We approach this through first defining a societal purpose for the brand on behalf of the consumer (a purpose that makes us proud). With the purpose defined, we ask ourselves, who do we need to 'be' to deliver it? What are the constituent parts of our character: our personality, attitudes, ethics, motivations, hopes, dreams and fears – what defines us? There are many techniques that we will discuss to help us build this brand feeling.

National Bank:

- **Purpose:** We are going back to the heart of banking: helping individuals, families and communities reach their fullest potential, through a supportive bank that personalises, simplifies and encourages the use of its products and services.
- **Character:** We are responsible and considered. We strive to be open and approachable, using simple, everyday language, and work hard to educate and advise our customers.

Digital Bank:

- **Purpose:** We want to change the nature of daily banking and embrace positive customer engagement.

- **Character:** We are a challenger, but not a revolutionary – an 'enlightened evolutionary'. Contemporary, social, customer-focused and energetically optimistic.

Core Concept 3: The Brand's Spirit

Cultural and consumer guidelines

We now bring everything together in defining the Brand's Spirit. We build a story around the purpose. What are the key internal beliefs and external character aspects of the brand that will help accomplish the brand's purpose? Again, a simple question, but as we will see, an inspirational process.

- **National Bank:** The role our brand plays in society is to help people, families and communities get the most out of our financial services.
- **Digital Bank:** The role our brand plays in society is to create a new concept in banking for a new age. We are unencumbered by the past and facilitated by modern attitudes and technology.

Application

The internal belief system and the external perception of the brand feeling need to be symbiotic, and together, create a perception of the Brand's Spirit. It should create a complete picture of internal motivations and external character that drive behaviour. The Brand's Spirit is the cultural and consumer social guidelines for what a brand is and/or will be.

As brand owners, we influence this spirit through every experience and interaction. Consumers find it simple to define brands through association, feelings and human characteristics. We need to have a comprehensive view of what we believe our Brand's Spirit is. We must be confident and informed enough to know how our brand will think and behave in any number of situations.

The applications internally are what drive the separation of the belief system to the brand feeling (although they have to work co-operatively). Human resource departments have found brand positioning to be unhelpful because it is not usually focused internally (staff) but externally (consumer). I believe the internal beliefs are as strong as external consumer purpose and brand character in shaping overall brand perception. This makes the process and its finding directly applicable to HR and/or cultural direction.

Side-stepping a potentially long and not critical debate, we value looking at the internal belief system of a brand's organisation separately to the brand's external 'feeling'. We also believe these should ultimately come together in the overall definition of the Brand's Spirit. In terms of expression, I favour expressing the consumer purpose and brand character in the final articulation of the Brand's Spirit, using the internal belief system as inspiration and guidance.

Modern marketing demands much more than consistency; brands must be honest, responsive and proactive. All of which is impossible unless the brand owner and all its partners have a shared understanding of the brand's beliefs, purpose and character: its spirit.

Defining Concepts: The Brand Story and the Brand Essence

FORMATIVE QUESTIONS	CORE CONCEPTS	DEFINING CONCEPTS
Our Heritage: Why was this brand created? Our Challenge: What is the key barrier to growth and profitability?	THE BRAND'S BUSINESS: The core business and its speciality or focus	The Brand Story: The confluence of the core concepts in a story The Brand Essence: A simple, familiar, emotionally engaging idea
Consumer Goal: What are the consumer goals within category? Brand Assets: What are the brand's strengths?	THE BRAND'S TRUTH: How we help the consumer achieve their goal	
Belief System: What cultural beliefs drive the brand? Brand Feeling: What are the brand's purpose and character?	THE BRAND'S SPIRIT: The cultural and consumer social guidelines	

The Defining Concepts are a summation of all of the Formative Questions and Core Concepts. It is split into two techniques. The first more elaborate, the second often agonisingly concise.

The Brand Story allows the benefit of more words. Using the Core Concepts as a guide, we can build the story of the brand. The power of a good story is obvious and well documented. The aim of this process is to positively influence how a consumer positions the brand in their own consciousness. As humans, we have used storytelling to remember, educate and influence since we have evolved. It is a tried and tested method to encapsulate the key elements of a brand. It gives all those who encounter it a reference point: an understanding of the business the brand is in, the goal it helps customers reach and the nature of the brand. With the fundamental parts we have created (the Core Concepts) and the convergent techniques we have used, it will be easy to create a small, insightful and concise Brand Story – no longer than 100 words and no 'white rabbits' (previously unmentioned new ideas or concepts).

> I resisted the Brand Story earlier in my career – preferring to use only the Brand Essence as a concluding statement. But the single-minded discipline required to develop a brand's essence can sometimes leave behind crucial elements of its story. I also became aware that past clients, in efforts to communicate an essence, had used approximations of their stories. I, therefore, saw the benefit of change.

The Brand Essence should flow from the Brand Story. Our ever-present philosophy of convergence dictates we now need to consolidate that story into one theme or idea, expressed in a one or two words or, at most, a single sentence.

It takes some considerable thought, creativity and a complete understanding of a brand to sum it up in a few words. But it is possible. One of my first mentors once imparted to me, 'Don't be clever, be clear' (thank you, Christine), and this advice is still the best I can pass on when developing a Brand Essence. It should be clear and concise and encapsulate the brand.

By way of explanation, the actual process a strategist goes through in the development of a 'strategic' Brand Essence is not unlike the development process for a 'creative brand line'. If you consider some of the best brand lines ever written, you can see how they encapsulate the brand in just a few words.

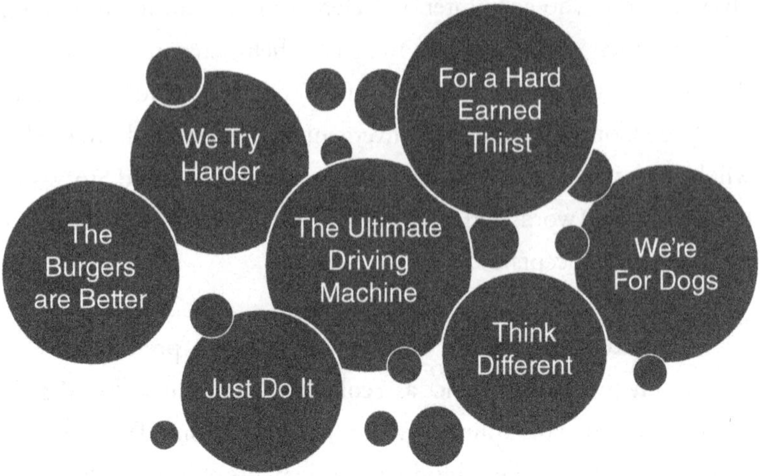

However, we are not writing a creative brand line (requiring engagement through creativity), we are writing a strategic Brand Essence (requiring understanding through clarity). This is not to say that the process does not require creativity because it does. Still, the execution (the words) should seek clarity over creativity. In my career, some of my own and my colleagues' Brand Essence lines have been used as brand lines. Sometimes strategic clarity and engaging creativity can be achieved – but rarely. My recommendation is to leave the brand and communications lines to the professional copywriters!

A Brand Essence is whatever we think it should be! I am not being misleading, just purposefully generic. A Brand's Essence is its 'DNA' or 'heart and soul'. It should be faithful to the product, motivate the customer and be distinct from the competition. Captured within a clear, concise single-minded statement. In this respect, *it is the absolute strategic confluence of the entire process.*

Process

I make no excuse for overuse of the terms 'convergent thinking' or 'causality' in this guide. The entire exercise of brand positioning is a process in the style of intellectual rigour, as is this final and crucial piece of the puzzle.

Each Formative Question will have multiple answers that we should converge into a single theme or idea, and then into a single Core Concept. The Core Concepts are used to create the final Defining Concepts: the Brand Story, which inspires the Brand Essence.

In art class, I was often told to 'paint what you see'; this advice is also applicable within this quasi-creative process. Do not reach for white rabbits. The best outcome when I present to my clients is 'of course that's what it should be!' Early in my career, I found this initially disappointing, but whether working on a start-up, established or challenger brand, you soon realise this is the ideal response. The individual or team responsible have gone on a journey together, and the outcome (no matter how inspiring, revolutionary or transformative) should seem like the most natural thing on earth.

As we progress with our banking example, without 'real-life' input, the process becomes more academic but still illustrative. To demonstrate the sequential nature of the process, we will recap our Formative Questions, Core Concepts and illustrate the brand's potential Brand Story and Brand Essences for our fictitious banks.

Bringing It Together 1: The National Bank Brand

Our Heritage
Established over 100 years ago, we have grown with the nation, supporting the individuals, communities and industry that built it.
Our Challenge
We are trusted yet lack connection. There is an absence of a simple, engaging and unifying theme across our services with which individuals and businesses can connect.
The Brand's Business
We provide access to a range of financial services across all of our customers' life stages.
Consumer Goal
Bank with trust, simplicity, familiarity and specialist expertise.
Brand Assets
We have an easily accessible, extensive product range. With the experience and expertise to advise you when and where you need it.
The Brand's Truth
As a market-leading brand, our customers benefit from our experience. To avoid becoming 'faceless', we provide personalised support for our customers. When you need us most in life, we will be there to offer the right advice.
Belief System
We believe in responsibility, understanding and expertise. Beliefs that guide us through the good and bad, boom and bust of our customers' lives and our nation's history.

Brand Feeling
Purpose: We are going back to the heart of banking: helping individuals, families and communities reach their fullest potential, through a supportive bank that personalises, simplifies and encourages the use of its products and services.
Character: We are responsible and considered. We strive to be open and approachable, using simple, everyday language, and work hard to educate and advise our customers.
The Brand's Spirit
The role our brand plays in society is to help people, families and communities get the most out of our financial services.
The Brand Story
We have grown with this nation, supporting the people who built it. Creating a broad range of products and services, easily available, to help achieve their financial goals whatever they are. Our broad experience and expertise mean we can guide our customers at times in their life when they need financial advice they trust. We want to get back to the heart of banking: to our customers, their families and communities. We will be human and open, using simple language, and will work hard to educate and be easily approachable. Making sure, when you need us most, we'll be there.
The Brand Essence
Helping people achieve what they want, when it matters most.

Bringing It Together 2: The Digital Bank Brand

Our Heritage
Created without the cumbersome infrastructures and bureaucracy of the traditional big banks, we offer a new, stripped-back banking model.
Our Challenge
We have yet to establish brand trust and longevity assurance. The competitive nature of our products and services have not been properly communicated. A reason for online-only banking, in an age of instant connection, is not well established.
The Brand's Business
We supply banking essentials at a low cost through all digital platforms.
Consumer Goal
A new way of banking, with tailored products and seamless delivery.
Brand Assets
We are flexible, active and customer orientated. We offer a new and different choice within the market.
The Brand's Truth
We won't appeal to large corporations or wealthy individuals, we will appeal to the new generation of digital, egalitarian, financial service customers. Our digital platform and the product and service essentials we offer allow greater simplicity, value and 24/7 customer service. We provide a new, straightforward and better value approach to banking.
Belief System
We believe in an agile and transparent approach. We are a digital innovator more than a bank, giving everyone access to the same great value products and services.

Brand Feeling
Purpose: We want to change the nature of daily banking and embrace positive customer engagement.
Character: We are a challenger, but not a revolutionary – an 'enlightened evolutionary'. Contemporary, social, customer-focused and energetically optimistic.
The Brand's Spirit
The role our brand plays in society is to create a new concept in banking for a new age. We are unencumbered by the past and facilitated by modern attitudes and technology.
The Brand Story
We are a contemporary approach to banking. We wanted to free ourselves from the traditional bricks and mortar and legacy systems and products of old banks. We provide, low-cost, essential financial products and services, through all digital and mobile channels. We offer fewer, more tailored life stage solutions to our customers. A new straightforward, simple and better value approach to banking. We are creating a new concept in banking for a new breed of customers. We are unencumbered by the past and facilitated by modern attitudes and technology. We are changing banking for the better.
The Brand Essence
Break-free Banking.

Application

In my consulting business, we have a tool we call 'True North' because it gives the brand direction – a continual reference and focal point for all the decisions made about the brand. The entire findings from this process can be taken and illustrated on a single page and given to everyone in the business as a single reference and source of inspiration. The results from this process give, first and foremost, clear brand definition and direction. It can bring together leadership teams, and provide common ground and understanding between management, staff and consumers. It never fails to inspire those who go through it, energising brands and businesses.

Over the years, clients have used the findings of the process in every conceivable aspect of their business. It has been used for new building design (often this process can guide architectural design) or re-designing an internal workspace. It has been used in recruitment and the development of internal cultural policies. It has been used (initially) to redefine a business's market (to grow or scale back). It has been used as the basis to stop the development of a product or service into a market. It is also used, more traditionally, by the business in the development of new products or services, as well as the fundamental marketing principles, influencing pricing, distribution and all forms of promotion. This process particularly lends itself to the digital age, acting as a brief in the development of digital strategy, experience and execution.

As you will have come to realise by now, the questions and concepts we arrive at throughout the process are not just an exercise in high-level strategic thinking but are relevant and applicable to the daily running of a business as well as the long-term success of a brand.

Over the coming chapters, we will now consider each Core Concept and its corresponding Formative Question in more depth, reflecting on these key areas:

- **The meaning and context**: Why we are asking this question and from what POV should we be answering.
- **Process and techniques used to explore the question**: People respond to questions in different ways, depending on how they are asked. Here we will give some examples of other 'ways in' to the same question.
- **Getting the right outcome**: Some clues, hints and general practical guidelines to what the answer should look like!

2

Core Concept 1: The Brand's Business

Our Heritage

Our Heritage: Why was this brand created?		
Meaning: Explore the brand's past, its original reason for creation and key formative moments through time.	**Process:** What are the creation story, the myths and legends, that surround the brand? Plot the critical events in the brand's history.	**Outcome:** An inspirational, often human, idea or theme, which encapsulates the human intent behind the business and how it shaped the brand.

Meaning

We want to explore the brand's past and identify key aspects, themes or ideas that naturally emerge, ultimately identifying a key theme that has been critical in shaping the brand. The more we understand the origin and developmental history, the better our understanding of the contemporary brand.

Brands are made over time; they are not instantly created. It doesn't matter whether it is a start-up or has been in the market for

100 years, a brand will have a creation story – a reason why it came into being. As a brand develops, there will be genuine catalysts in its history, moments in time where it has changed direction, refocused or evolved. The creation story and these events are the key evolutionary 'ingredients' in the brand's heritage that this Formative Question seeks to identify and articulate into a unifying theme.

As we are exploring the brand's history, heritage and reason for creation, these questions need to be kept firmly in the past, so a historical point of view is applied. We also want to know from a business point of view what have been the formative, key events that have shaped the brand. So, we should frame the context for the questions and answers from a business, not a consumer, point of view.

Process

A little preparation can go a long way here, especially if you are working with a brand with a long history. However, we shouldn't over-intellectualise. The beauty of this guide is simplicity. What we remember about our brand without researching is what we want to record. As the leaders in this exercise, we should have a detailed knowledge of the history of the brand, but what is immediately remembered is often what is most useful. However, revisiting forgotten aspects of the past and re-entering them back into the company psyche can also be helpful.

Why was this brand created?

Here, moderation skills need to be employed because we want the emotional rather than the rational response. We want to know the reason the brand was created beyond profit and revenue. This line of questioning can sometimes be personal, especially with the creators of the brand – so exercise empathy and intuition here as well as tenacity if working within a group.

Often this question focuses on an original idea or a different way of doing things that previously hadn't existed – rich seams for the overall positioning. It can also focus on the original dreams, desires and needs of the creators of the product or service. It is frequently, therefore, an inspiring conversation.

Often, the original creators of the brand have long since left, or the business has developed into something different through successive mergers and acquisition. I would always recommend seeking out the original creators or at least gaining an understanding of their initial intentions. Brands are a product of their experience, and like children, significant imprints are left early in their lives. To truly understand a brand, we must understand its childhood! If the business in question has seen successive development, we must focus on the brand. We need to follow the brand (not the business) back through time to understand its growth and the intentions of that growth as best as we can.

What are the stories, myths and legends that surround the brand?
One of my favourite exercises in this Formative Question is asking about myths, legends and stories of the brand. Like many of the techniques in this process, it has emerged from experience. I have regularly noticed that when a group of brand owners, boards or management teams became animated and engaged with this part of the process, they are recounting brand myths and legends.

Like all myths and legends, there are always some facts in the mix. But in this case, perception is reality. It doesn't matter whether they are true or not; the internal stories about the development of a brand are compelling. They often shine a light on a key theme or idea that is recurrent in the brand's history – precisely what we are looking for in this question.

What are the key events in the brand's history?

There are formative experiences, key episodes in everyone's lives, and those experiences make them who they are. Brands work in the same way. So, let's look at those experiences.

Creating a timeline of significant events, annotating the breakthroughs, the changes in direction, the growth, the decline and the refocusing can help highlight these episodes. Then, we need to determine what stands out most and why.

Developing a historical timeline is not too exciting and doesn't work practically within a group, so it's important we don't get bogged down in the details. It is sometimes a good idea to have one already prepared if working in a group. If working alone – remember this is not a complete, historically accurate piece of research. We are looking for significant moments, the things people usually remember. Events that have been forgotten have often been forgotten for a reason!

We need to be careful not to stray into the present, or we may start answering a question that is best tackled later.

Outcome

In my experience, if you dig hard enough into the history of a brand, there is always inspiration that proves vital to the overall Brand Story and Brand Essence. Even for brands that are not yet in the market, there will be a reason the creators are doing what they are doing beyond financial success.

Within this question, we are looking for a single thought, idea or theme that has been significant in shaping the brand. It will be the confluence of understanding the reason for creation and/or the key defining moments in the brand's history. Within this question, we want a single thought that encapsulates the themes.

The question is posed from a 'business historical' point of view. It therefore needs to be answered as such. It is surprising how honest the answers are if we follow the techniques illustrated for the questions. This is the benefit of the model – asking small questions to build big concepts!

I have found the best answers for this question come from the creation story, the reason (beyond money) the brand was established. The band creation story is often very personal in nature and is therefore always engaging as a result. It can refocus a brand on its true heritage. Often, with the fast pace (short-term-ism) of modern business development, a brand can lose its 'sense of self'. This process is often fundamental in finding the way forward. Even the simple process of walking through the key changes in the brand and understanding why those changes were made, is a rich source of inspiration.

The pitfall here is 'control' if we are in a group, or 'discipline' if we are on our own. The questions naturally roll from one to another – they are designed that way! It is tempting to begin discussing these findings and applying them to the present; however, when that happens, go back to the beginning.

Essentially, we are asking the business to look at the past and derive the key aspects, events and developments that shaped the brand. Consider those aspects, and develop a thought that encapsulates or is a recurrent theme within the answers. Express that theme in a single-minded and straightforward way.

By way of universal example, having already used banks, I will now look at competitive airlines. In this fictitious example, let us take a national carrier airline, established and well-known. In our other example, let's consider a budget airline, one that is relatively new, born from the price-challenger trend within the category.

- **National Carrier heritage:** Our history is linked to that of the national development of aviation. We played a large role in the development of this category. From a few fledgling planes in the early 1900s, a national fleet has developed, servicing the largest number of national and international locations.

- **Summarised heritage:** We played a significant role in the development of aviation in our country, helping connect people locally and nationally, and linking our country with the rest of the world.

From this, you can see how history can birth overall brand positionings and communication campaigns. British Airways used this as an advertising platform for their iconic 'Bringing people together' advertisement and brand platform through the 1990s.

- **Budget Airline heritage:** We have developed over the last 20 years into a well-established low-fare airline. Competing with major international airlines, we built our business on creating new routes to popular national and near-by international locations. We fought hard to gain access to these routes, battling established carriers and governments to maintain and grow our service. We don't always fly from the major airports in the markets we serve, but we always offer a lower cost than major international and full-service airlines. We pride ourselves on being a people's champion – keeping overheads low and passing that on to the customer through low-cost fares.
- **Summarised heritage:** We are a challenger brand, a rebel prepared to take on the establishment in creating and growing a low-fare airline.

Expressing the answer is always subjective and a matter of 'what feels right is right'. In this question, I find it useful to focus on the human spark of inspiration that led to the creation. Why people start businesses is often more personal and emotive than rational. This question is usually more focused on the 'heart'. The next question is more focused on the 'head'.

Our Challenge

Our Challenge: What is the key barrier to growth and profitability?		
Meaning: Explore the present-day business context to understand the nature of the brand challenge.	**Process:** Identify brand barriers through 5P's & PESTEL frameworks. Why are we here? View brand lifecycle and competition.	**Outcome:** Define the brand's key business challenge(s) expressed as a simple articulation of the key issue or barrier to growth.

Meaning

Here, we are exploring the business environment and context that the brand exists within today. We are determining the key challenges to the brand that impede growth. This is answered from a 'business point of view'. There are many challenges to running a business, but there are always crucial issues that are either top of mind or perceived to be significant barriers (usually both!). They could be evident within the internal or external perception of the product or service, the manufacturing, distribution, pricing, ranging or packaging, but may involve the changing social, market or consumer dynamics. There are no limits to what can be perceived as key challenges.

When ultimately positioning a brand, it must be accomplished with an understanding of the critical issues within the business that impact its profit or growth. It is useful to remember this is not an operational, fiscal or business strategy meeting. (In my consultancy, I cover this question with the key members of the team individually, prior to any workshop).

We need to remain as 'top-level' as possible when considering the key business challenges (today) for the brand overall, and not get lost in the minutia!

Process

What are the key barriers impeding growth and profitability? Looking at a brand's positioning strategy often denotes the need for some sort of evolution due to societal, product, market or consumer challenges – and we typically know what they are.

If you don't know, you will need to spend some time here establishing the context for your brand positioning. Having different members of the team present is vital in this instance. Most businesses (dependent on size) will have some form of finance, sales, category, marketing or management representation. Gathering these representatives together and asking what your business challenges are is a rewarding exercise in itself. Each specialisation usually brings to the table their own concerns – and working through the groups' concerns, universal challenges will often emerge.

There are various frameworks we can employ to bring out and decide the key brand challenges. Utilise the classic 4P's (Product, Price, Place and Promotion), or, preferably, the 5P's (by adding People). Or try PESTEL, looking at the macro business challenges through Political, Economic, Social, Technological, Environmental and Legal filters.

Is the business a start-up, established, challenger or iconic brand? This could be obvious, or it could lead to debate. Establishing and agreeing on what stage a brand is in from a business point of view is useful in determining the overall Brand Story and Brand Essence (e.g. a brand strategy for a new brand is usually different from an established one). A challenger brand has a different approach to the iconic #1 brand. Still, the discussion may prompt the desired change in brand approach – the iconic brand wants to become the challenger; the established brand wants to act like a start-up, or the start-up has matured and needs an appropriate strategy.

Why are we here?

Avoiding the philosophical responses(!), there is often an underlying reason the brand has come under review. It is always essential to get that reason on the table as soon as possible. For example: something wrong or great has happened; something important has changed (political, economic, social, technological, environmental, legal, or in leadership); an opportunity or market has opened or closed.

One of the significant barriers to a successful brand definition is modern business politics. The reason a brand often remains undefined (or at least open to interpretation) is to allow the necessary degree of ambiguity. Necessary, because it will enable all the senior brand executives to agree. Although politically expedient, this is often why brands stagnate (or worse). Brands are like people: wear your heart on your sleeve, and people know what you stand for.

You have to be honest in this process with yourself, the team and the business.

How do we compare with the competition?

Often, a challenge or an advancement by the competition will necessitate a response or change in direction. In this section, we are not looking for a full competitive review. But, if necessary, we must identify the challenge the competition has forced us to consider.

Once we have thoroughly explored this question, there may be several challenges. In my experience, there is often a recurrent theme. It may exhibit itself in different ways but come from the same source. We need to spend some time discarding minor irritants, and sorting and grouping reoccurring themes, through reference back to the original question. The goal is to establish a single key challenge. However, we can settle for a maximum of three challenges that are impeding the brand's success.

Outcome

This question, more than any other, is quite specific and will have answers based on the understanding of the marketplace, the consumer and the brand itself. It directs our thinking towards those challenges that are an impediment for growth. It is ultimately an introductory question – the answers set the context for the Core Concept to be answered. Hence, the answers to this question are usually more contextual – they help frame the answer and are not the answer itself.

Critical again in this process is convergence. Many impediments come from a reoccurring barrier. Looking at all the challenges, barriers and threats on a page, consider the similarities – trace back the stated challenges, barriers or threats. Is there a similar origin? Remember, we don't have to get to three – Ideally, we should get one. Three is a maximum, not a minimum. Then, try to articulate the key challenge using plain language versus business terminology. In doing this, it will be easier to capture multiple business issues into a single brand problem.

For example, I often hear, 'We're losing what we were through growth, so we need to capture and define what that was before we lose it completely'. Or from the growth cycle of the brand, 'We have been the same size for years; we don't know how to grow'; and 'We have grown as a business, come of age. We need our brand to reflect this'. Newer brands might say, 'We are a new brand, we must simply tell people what we do and why they should support us'; or 'We want to expand to the next level, and we need a brand that can take us there'.

The challenge can be people-based, 'Our own people are not engaging as much with the brand as they used to'; or 'We are a new team; we need to set a common agenda for the brand'. Or product-based, 'We have so many product lines we need to define what exactly we are'.

Key challenges also result from the category and the consumer. We typically hear, 'The market (or) our competition has moved the goalposts, and we no longer believe we're in the right territory'; or 'We are no longer as relevant to our customer base. We need to give them a reason to reengage and reassess us'.

This is obviously not an exhaustive list, but even from these few examples, we can understand the nature of the challenge.

To continue our specific airline examples:

- **National Carrier challenges:** How does a legacy brand remain relevant within a competitive national carrier context? The technological revolution has democratised air travel, making price comparison easy and increasingly influential in consumer decision-making. A national airline is no longer the default consumer choice, but one of many options. Increased competition from low-cost domestic and international brands are stealing volume share.
- **Summarised challenge:** A National airline is no longer the default consumer choice. How do we maintain our volume share in an increasingly competitive market?
- **Budget Airline challenges:** The technological revolution has democratised air travel, making price comparison easy and increasingly influential in consumer decision-making. Major airlines can compete with 'fare sales' to and from major airports. Yet, we operate at such low margins, we are vulnerable to global fuel costs, geo-political tensions and natural disasters. We also

face increased competition from low-cost international brands entering our market and stealing share. The brand needs to attract and continue to attract large volumes of customers to sustain the business model. We need to create a positioning for ourselves that differentiates us from other low-cost airlines (particularly as we grow).

- **Summarised challenge:** Everyone in our category can be 'budget'. We need to be more to continue to be attractive and survive.

From these examples, we can see how by grouping together what are often business challenges (expressed with business language), we can summarise them into every day, plain language. And that is all we need from this question. We have our contextual challenges; time to move on.

The Brand's Business

The Brand's Business: The core business and its speciality or focus		
Meaning: We want to find the best definition of our brand's commercial role and focus within the defined category.	**Process:** Consider the past heritage, the challenges today and competition in defined category. Within a commercial context describe the core business and the business core speciality.	**Outcome:** A simple expression of a complex concept. A future-proofed definition of the core business: What we do. And the key business focus: What we are good at (vs Competition).

Meaning

This Core Concept is defined by utilising the Formative Questions as a platform for inspiration. Here, we explore the past and the present to decide the future, considering the past business heritage and the current business challenges to define the future business role for the brand. Simply put (and avoiding much practical and academic debate), we want to find the best definition of our brand's commercial role and focus within the defined category.

There are three strategic considerations (or nuances) here, which I have avoided so far in this book for fear of over-complication. However, I feel that discussing them here will add clarity to this simple sounding, but quite often complex, Core Concept.

Firstly, if brands exist in consumers' heads, we should consider the consumer motivation within the category (the next section) first and foremost. I believe any brand positioning strategy needs to be loyal to the product or service and the business. Hence, we could create any brand positioning – even a perfect one – but if it is not faithful to the business, it will fail. If the business claims 'full-service', 'low cost', 'healthy', 'family values' or 'customer first', it must be in a commercial position to deliver those things. This is why we focus on gaining insight and defining the Brand's Business first.

Secondly, as marketers, entrepreneurs and just good business-people, we will be looking for a consumer insight or benefit of our brand to promote. This is only natural, but it is critical to approach the Brand's Business Core Concept from a commercial point of view. Considering the commercial context for our brand, how might we describe the business the brand is in and its focus? One technique outlined next asks us to consider our focus against competitors. This places the business within the commercial and not consumer context. Here are some fictitious examples of core business focus for illustration.

- If we are a bank, do we seek to give a comprehensive service of products through nationally available stores, or are we supplying essential consumer products online only?
- If we sell pasta, how are we distinct from other pasta brands? Is it fresh or dried? Are we international, local or an importer? Are we a new or heritage brand? Do we specialise in ingredients or focus on food trends?
- If we are a restaurant, compared with the competitive set, how might we define ourselves? Via national style – Ethiopian, Thai, Chinese – or do we push contemporary fusion? Are we family-friendly, quick-service or high-end dining? Is our focus locally sourced produce, sharing plates, diffident or gregarious service?
- If we sell furniture, are we online only? Do we use recycled materials? Is our business prestige focused, handcrafted, or mass-produced, focused on lower cost?
- If we work in real estate, is our business local, national or global, independent or part of a network or franchise? What makes our business distinct from the competition, lower or fixed commission, faster or higher sales, integrated services or customer service?

Now, let's consider this last aspect of a common business focus, customer service. In a modern marketing age, with little product differentiation, one common (initial) brand positioning area is around 'customer first'. A Brand's Business can focus on customer service, but like consistency, good service is mostly a given. In very few cases, like the Avis of old and FedEx of today, service can be demonstrably different to the competition, and so can be useful to include as a focus unpacked within the next Core Concept.

However, we can't use this option as a 'fall back' or 'usual suspect'. The core business aspect should describe 'what we do'. The business focus aspect should explain 'how we do it' differently or distinctly from the competitors.

Thirdly, in terms of definition. Within this guide, when I refer to 'a Brand's Business' we are seeking to define the role of that brand commercially and articulate its focus within the competitive category. This is separate and different to articulating the business strategy within the marketplace. This is a brand, not a business strategy model. Business strategy is more concerned with making money than building brands. However, obviously, one way of making money is building a strong brand, so the two strategies do and should overlap. But business strategy should always lead brand strategy. It is impossible or at least inadvisable to try and formulate a brand strategy without a firm business strategy already in place.

We are more concerned with description, definition, and then the focus of the existing business the brand is in – identifying and focusing on what is already there.

In some cases, however, the current role of the brand may be commercially unsatisfactory. It might be spread too thin, its focus might be too narrow, it could have become obsolete or less salient. This is one of the reasons we include the 'Our Challenge' section within this Core Concept.

Hence, when determining the outcome for this Core Concept, we first need to understand if the current role of the brand is the best. Once this is decided, we can then consider the competition within that category and define our focus to complete our definition.

Process

We must first ask ourselves a critical question: 'What is our business focus (for the brand) now, and what do we want it to be in the future?' A pretty important question! One with the power to transform our brand (and potentially the business).

Considering our heritage, is there a mismatch between what the brand was and what it is today? Either way, it is worth consideration. We may decide the evolved state of the brand is justified and use the past to influence, or nudge, the direction of the future. Considering the defined summary of the brand's heritage, are there other opportunities on the table? Can we take this learning about our brand and apply it to other categories or even markets? Is there potential for any vertical or horizontal expansion opportunity? The opposite is sometimes also true: can we refocus on a core range of products? Having identified the brand's original focus, it may be that it has lost its way or expanded too far, signalling a need to return to its core.

Considering our key business challenge, the size, scope and potential impact of the challenge may make the current business less attractive. We may have to expand, contract or jump into new markets and categories because of the insurmountable nature of our challenges.

However, brands seldom need dramatic change; often a slight shift in focus or reframing can nudge them back on course. Often the products (or at least core products) will remain unchanged, but the brand itself will need to evolve.

This question is vital. We should embrace the chaos that might follow! It will either confirm and define the current focus, or one element will evolve in some way. If this happens, fantastic; spend some time defining the newly developed category (from a business point of view) and the new evolved business focus within that category.

Whatever happens, the question facilitates an exciting debate about what exactly the brand should or should not focus on. With the core business focus initially explored and defined, we can now consider the competition in that category to determine the focus.

'How do the competitive set define their business, and how do they describe their brand's focus?'

From a strategic point of view, it is obviously a good idea to build a picture of what our competition is doing, not least because this is the market environment and consumer perceptual context in which your brand will ultimately be assessed. It is useful to consider how the other brands in our desired competitive set describe their business. A simple shortcut is through some analysis of competitor websites. In viewing these sites, we can usually determine how they summarise their business and focus. Their definition and approach will be evident in any information they offer about themselves, their history, what they do, and the products or services they offer.

We are not looking for the competition's brand positioning in this exercise. We are looking at the way they describe the business they are in, and what they are particularly good at. Identify themes, trends and ideas in the way they talk about their business and business focus.

With the results, we can again make an informed decision. We will have a frame of reference for how the competition describes their brand. We should be led by the process to define our Brand's Business, but we should do it with the knowledge of how the competitors within our category describe themselves.

Outcome

The process within this Core Concept is driving us towards a simplistic and clear summary definition of our Brand's Business and focus or speciality. The nature of the exercise will allow the previous questions around heritage, key challenges, desired business and competitor definition to permeate our answer.

If we were to gather business partners, colleagues, departments or board members together and ask them 'What is the core business and focus of our brand?' The answer would seldom be the same. In fact, the answer is often very different. Getting the right answer is, therefore, tricky. In fact, it is probably the most difficult within this process!

The answer should be concise and clear. We are seeking clarity over cleverness. Define 'our core business' and 'our business focus' – once we have these elements, we have the pieces to create the Core Concept: The Brand's Business. Definition of terms is critical here so let's explore the definitions and some potential answers to illustrate the theory.

Core Business

There is always historical business language to cover different business areas within small or large brands. If you gather together all the products and services that the brand offers, how might we talk about them?

At this early stage in the process, we should say what we see. We don't want to overcomplicate this answer. While I have seen this Core Concept fundamentally change the focus of brands and their associated business, most of the time, the answer is obvious. But subtleties in definition, at this stage, make a big difference later. For example, I am often asked to run through this process for marketing service agencies. In their continually changing landscape, this is often a Core Concept that causes great debate.

This is a timely point for discussion around the varying importance of each Core Concept. The process is sequential; hence, each Core Concept is important, but for each of the hundreds of brands I have worked with, one concept becomes more important in terms of the final answer (the Brand Story and Brand Essence). If this section provides a breakthrough moment, then it could well be the catalyst for change for the brand. If it is obvious (and you are sure you have been rigorous) then move on – the breakthrough will be within the other Core Concepts.

The definition of the brand's business within marketing service companies is as complex as it is critical. Twenty years ago, an advertising agency did pretty much everything: client services, creative, production and media planning, and buying. Now, through successive fragmentation, we can pretty much find a specialist for every one of these services, and the services themselves have splintered into specialist areas. Added to this, there has been a revolutionary change with the introduction of digital and social platforms, resulting not just in further fragmentation of services but in muddying the waters of responsibility. When considering agencies, clients often ask me, 'Where exactly do you go to get this service?' And further, 'Where does their role start and stop?' Hence, for a modern marketing agency, defining their focus and the scope of their services (the Brand's Business) is fundamental to their and their clients' understanding of who they are and what they do.

An advertising agency could be full-service (e.g. strategy, creative, digital, design and media), specialist (e.g. brand identity), traditional (focused on client service), this is rare, though I have seen it work, or contemporary (e.g. only working with technology brands or digital based communications). Or – and here we get to the point – as is the modern fashion, 'customer experience' agencies. Hence, their Brand's Business definition is the provision of customer experiences (through all or some of these services). When we consider the overall category, there is always the right definition that gives the brand the freedom to be everything we want it to be.

Business Focus

If the Brand's Business is the commercial definition of the business, the brand's focus is the speciality within the desired commercial context. We therefore need to identify the business focus of our brand within our desired category.

Larger, often older brands will have expanded over time to offer a full range. Smaller, often younger brands will be very focused. But there will (or should) be a singular commercial focus.

Another way to think about this question is, what is the brand's commercial 'claim to fame?' Or, what does it do commercially well or better than the competition? In a workshop context, I sometimes also ask the question in reverse, 'What would this category be missing if you didn't exist?' People's brains work in different ways. It is a constant within the workshop context that you repeat the same questions in different ways – allowing everyone to comprehend and respond.

Reducing a large and iconic or small or new brand to a single commercial focus is not easy. However, be led by the process. It may be obvious, and it may take work. The result will be liberating, or at least satisfying.

For illustration, let's take some globally recognised brands (brands I have had no direct contact with) and, using information within the public domain, let's see how they express their core business and business focus.

The following examples are interpreted corporate and/or brand statements from the public domain.

Danone

'We have become a world leader in four businesses: Essential Dairy and Plant-Based Products, Early Life Nutrition, Medical Nutrition and Waters. Building on a unique health-focused portfolio that allows us to be a key player in the food revolution.'

Here we have a sophisticated example of a global multi-faceted food company, succinctly describing its business and focus. The core business is the 'Health-focused portfolio', and the business focus is the ... 'a key player in the food revolution'. This is a commercial, not a customer, benefit. But you can see how a well-defined brand business can give clear direction for a brand overall.

(Danone website. Retrieved June 2020, from: https://www.danone.com/about-danone/at-a-glance/our-businesses.)

Google

Google's business is...

'...to organize the world's information and make it universally accessible and useful.'

Unsurprisingly, considering its success, Google has always had an impressive grasp of its brand strategy. Its core business is organising the world's information; the focus is to make it accessible and useful.

(Google global website. Retrieved June 2020, from: https://www.google.com/search/howsearchworks/mission.)

Toyota

'Toyota will lead the future mobility society, enriching lives around the world with the safest and most responsible ways of moving people.'

Toyota is not in car manufacturing – they are in the business of mobility. Their focus: moving people safely and responsibly. This is an excellent illustration of the increased scope a well-defined brand business can bring.

(Global Toyota website. Retrieved June 2020, from: https://global.toyota/en/company/vision-and-philosophy)

IKEA

'Our business idea... to offer a wide range of well-designed, functional home furnishing products at prices so low that as many people as possible will be able to afford them.'

The core business of IKEA is a wide range of well-designed functional home furnishings, and its focus is low price and affordability.

(IKEA Global website. Retrieved June 2020, from: https://www.ikea.com/au/en/this-is-ikea/about-us/vision-and-business-idea)

Virgin

'Virgin is known for challenging the status quo – taking on industry giants and championing people and the planet.'

I've always been a big fan of this brand's business definition, although for many years it was a given and not articulated. Now, as they say, 'Disruption is in our DNA'. As a brand, this is what Virgin has always done, and I presume this is the premise for expansion; the Brand's Business is 'challenging the status quo', its focus is 'taking on industry giants and championing the people'.

(Virgin Global website. Retrieved June 2020, from: https://www.virgin.com/virgingroup/content/our-purpose)

I have tried to stay with analysis through publicly available materials to illustrate the method discussed. When we are looking for our own definition of the Brand's Business, we can easily conduct online research, to some degree, to review the category and competitors. If we are the competition (or even in the same category) to these examples, inspiration and understanding can be found from reviewing them.

Within our process, the actual expression should be a short statement that reflects the two elements outlined. In this section, we are seeking clarity, not differentiation.

The answer is logical and sequential, hence inescapable. We sometimes find some similarity with competitors; this is not unusual and is expected within this section. The expression of the answer is up to us. It is here we can seek differentiation if we find ourselves with the exact same definition as our leading competitor. But we shouldn't seek to change the essence of our findings: our brand is what it is.

To close, let's consider our fictitious examples. In our two banking examples the Brand's Business was: 'providing access to a range of financial services across all of our customers' life stages' and, 'supplying banking essentials at low cost through all digital platforms'. In other words, what they do and want to focus on.

Utilising our airline examples to illustrate the Brand's Business will give further clarity:

- **National Carrier Brand's Business:** We are the nation's airline. We offer a full range of high-frequency flights both domestically and internationally across the country and to the rest of the world's major airports. We provide the very best on-ground and in-air service for our customers.
- **Summarised Brand's Business:** We are the nation's airline, providing a full-service solution to domestic and international locations.
- **Budget Airline Brand's Business:** We provide an alternative to major international airlines. Selling basic fares, with optional extras, allows us to offer lower-cost services than the other major airlines.
- **Summarised Brand's Business:** We fly regular low-cost flights to a selection of domestic and international destinations.

These are just examples to illustrate the questions and potential answers. But hopefully, the difference already created in the strategic journeys of the brands is obvious. By enforcing simplicity, through sacrifice and focus, we have identified the business we are in and our focus. This has tremendous potential within the current and future focus of every aspect of our business.

3

Core Concept 2: The Brand's Truth

Consumer Goal

Consumer Goal: What are the consumer goals within the category?		
Meaning: The universal needs and higher motivations that drive preference and brand choice within our brand's category.	**Process:** Research, market mapping and 'laddering' techniques will identify deeper motivation, drivers or consumer goals within categories.	**Outcome:** Understand the motivations and goals of the consumer within your category. Identify 2–4 key consumer goals within the category.

Meaning

Now that we have considered our heritage, challenges and our desired core business and focus (the Brand's Business), we are now ready to consider our consumer. It is the consumer, after all, who will position the brand in their own head (with our help!). Therefore, within this section, we are answering the questions from a consumer point of view (in the previous section, we were answering from a business or commercial point of view). We are asking this customer question at a category (not brand) level.

Theoretical note:

There is much debate over the role of the target audience in defining a brand strategy. To understand our approach, I will try to summarise the debate.

Historically, communications strategy was based around an understanding and insight into a specific or single target audience (leading to a proposition for specific communication).

Brand strategy was less focused on the specific customer and more on the overall brand, which usually has more than one customer segment. Most sophisticated marketing organisations will operate complex 'target audience segmentation'. This method uses quantitative data and statistical analysis that puts customers into different groups based on who they are, their attitudes and purchasing behaviour. So, any single brand like McDonald's or Mars might have seven or more key customer segments.

Hence, the debate. Do you focus on specific customers or all customers within your brand strategy development? Added to this, and probably because of this question, a third method became popular; an 'idealised customer segment'. Essentially, making up who you think your best customer segment would be.

The sequential nature of this model now begins to help guide us through the process. In the previous Core Concept, we defined our commercial category and our focus. This will give guidance as to the category target. It is within this category target that we need to understand and identify the consumer goals and motivation.

Concerning the debate mentioned, we are not focusing on a single or idealised target customer group, or even the multiple groups that are the brand's customers. *We are focusing on the prescribed category customers.* For example, let's think about the banking brands already used.

- For the **National Bank** brand, we articulated, 'We provide access to a range of financial services across all of our customers' life stages.' This, therefore, would define our category customer broadly – anyone with financial needs through their life. Motivated by trust, security and advice.
- For the **Digital Bank** brand, we articulated, 'We supply banking essentials at a low cost through all digital platforms.' This, therefore, would define our category customer more narrowly – digitally comfortable, desiring better customer experience and value. Accepting of modern brands and lifestyle choices.

The conclusion to the Brand's Business guides us towards our category customer. If the Brand's Business is broad, we may consider the entire category our target. If it is more selective, we will be able to introduce qualifiers. Still, we should always make the category customer as broad as possible.

This is a guide; every brand needs to be treated separately and in its own right. It is easy to overcomplicate with strategic debate. Suffice to say, in choosing a core business and focus, you will naturally gravitate to a category customer, where you can explore multiple consumer goals.

Process

We are all subject to the same basic internal and external motivations. Internally, we all develop attitudes and values based on experience.

Often those values are universal – our ideas of family, society, politics, success and failure. Those values influence our opinion and actions. In the same way, externally, we are sensitised to how people will perceive and judge us, based on what we do, wear, live, think and say. Categories always exhibit key drivers based on human motivation.

What is our consumer's motivation?

Within brand strategy, we are more concerned with emotive drivers over rational points of difference. There is increasing academic evidence (gathered through Behavioural Economics, Neuromarketing and Psychology) that would suggest most decisions are made, at least initially, from intuition and emotion. Therefore, it would be quite natural to extend this to purchase decisions. The more positively engaged (how much we like something), the greater the propensity (when the opportunity presents itself) to buy.

> There is a great deal of fascinating academic and popular literature around this topic. Starting points: read anything by Antonio Damasio; put *Thinking, Fast and Slow*, by Daniel Kahneman on your reading list for the full story, mix with Malcolm Gladwell's *Blink* for the shorter version. A personal favourite is Rory Sutherland, who founded Ogilvy's behavioural science practice (listen to any TED Talks!).

Consumer goals exist at a basic level (to drink, eat, sleep), and at a more complex needs level (status, security, love or ultimately self-actualisation). *To explore this further, research Maslow's Hierarchy of Needs.* Most companies build their brand strategy against an understanding of their consumer's deeper, more complex motives (or should do!).

The customer is, of course, usually buying something to satisfy a rational or functional need (food, car, clothes). However, which brand they choose is motivated by that brand's capability to match or relate to their personal motivation and goals.

Finally, and I have tried to find the attribution of this quote for many years to no avail, it may just have become or has always been a marketing truism: 'If you want to sell something, find out why people buy it!' The key to creating a positive brand positioning is to first understand the motivations and goals of the consumer that lead to the purchase.

What are our consumer goals?

Brand strategy requires a particular and often deeper level of thinking about the product and service, and no more so than within this question. Here are some techniques to help arrive at the category consumer motivation and subsequently, their goals.

Research – Understanding a category customer comes more naturally to some companies than others. But most successful companies have an intuitive knowledge of their consumer, and it is an effortless thing to develop with a little research. Hire research companies, talk to the sales teams or get out in the field (lurking around the POS)! There are numerous cost-effective ways to understand our customer. The key point when considering the research within this context is to build an understanding of why a category customer buys from a particular brand. We need to understand our consumer purchasing motivation within our customer category.

There are two key aspects to understanding this question. Firstly, we must understand the brand perception for both the business and our competitors (remember, they are buying, initially at least, based on emotion and intuition). Secondly, we must understand the purchase process. What is their primary need, their initial consideration, the moment of truth (purchase), and post-purchase experience? At each of these stages, we need to explore the physical process and personal goals to be satisfied.

Market mapping – Mapping is a handy tool (when used correctly). Naturally, brands evolve over time to fill consumer needs through the laws of supply and demand. When we see a 'gap' in the market, we try and 'fill' it.

Let's take something we should all do: eat more fruit. Within this category, there are various motivations at work, which all result in a purchase. Firstly, most people will have a standard set of fruits they purchase regularly. They may also buy what is on special because they are value-conscious (or have a large family of fruit-guzzling children!). In opposition, some buy only expensive, premium brands. They may buy on taste. They may buy for health, favouring antioxidants versus sugar. If we grew fruit, we would have to understand the range of motivations and goals our consumer processes in their purchase decision.

A simple way to understand the scope of customer motivation is to plot the parameters in opposition to each other. As a shortcut, you could use the previous competitive analysis outlined in the first Core Concept. Develop an understanding of the consumer goals the competitor brands are trying to target by a simple review of their websites and apply that knowledge within a consumer, not commercial context.

Laddering techniques – Laddering is a simple technique that will help in determining the answer to this question. I was taught this technique through the Account Planning Group (APG) early in my career in London. (I can find no specific academic reference to the method but have taught it myself and seen it used in many agencies and client organisations since.)

Like all useful tools, the laddering technique is simple and universal. Within this context, we will use it to 'ladder up' product or service attributes into product and then consumer benefits, giving us category consumer goals.

For the sake of a universal example, let us consider toothpaste. The category has many different subcategories: children's, sensitive, and whitening varieties. Let's utilise these to illustrate (some oversimplified) examples of laddering:

- Children's toothpaste: the products include cartoon endorsements or sparkling gel (product attributes) that lead to the experience being fun (product benefit), with the consumer benefit of establishing good oral hygiene in children for parents.
- Sensitive toothpaste: the products put a protective layer over teeth (product attribute) that leads to reduced sensitivity (product benefit), with the consumer benefit of eating and drinking what you want.
- Whitening toothpaste: the products use whitening dentistry products (product attribute) that lead to whiter teeth (product benefit), with the consumer benefit of greater social confidence.

From a brand positioning view, it's clear why many brands ultimately ladder up to confidence within this category.

By a simple process of laddering, we can take any product or service and explore some of the category consumer motivations that will, in turn, give a better understanding of broader consumer goals.

One more example I use in workshops is the pen someone is holding. The conversation usually goes like this:

'What are the product attributes of this pen?'

'It's got black ink, ballpoint (or nib), a screw top (or retractable), a rubber grip.'

'Now, what is the product benefit of *your* pen?'

'Well, it writes.'

'Exactly.' (I also explore other product benefits here, e.g. writing easily, smoothly, doesn't slip, doesn't clog or blotch)

'What is the benefit of writing?'

'It helps me record information and ideas, my thoughts, things to do.' Looking at me strangely and now slightly nervous.

'What's the benefit of recording information?' Opening it up to the workshop. 'Passing on knowledge.'

'What is the benefit of passing on knowledge?'

'Learning, education, not making the same mistakes, evolution, world peace?'

Now, I am not suggesting Bic, for example, should articulate its consumer goal as world peace! In this example, I bring the key product benefit back to writing and focus on the consumer benefits of this, as articulated here, 'It helps me record information and ideas, my thoughts, things to do'.

I believe this is the best territory for the consumer goal for this product. A good pen is, in fact, the starting point of many ideas.

Outcome

This Formative Question is contextual. It forces consideration of the consumer and category, not the brand. The next Formative Question focuses on specific brand strengths. Resist the temptation at this point to answer a different question, 'How does our brand help the consumer in our category?' A perfectly good question, but one we will answer later in this chapter, within the Brand's Truth.

Categories have generic motivation needs and associated goals. Every product or service starts with a basic need – to eat, sleep, travel, have fun or relax. But they can all be laddered up to find the broad category consumer goals using the techniques previously illustrated.

For example (evident in our previous bank examples), most of our financial services and products have been built around retail banks. Most of us need (not necessarily want) mortgages, credit and debit cards. Like it or not, banks facilitate our living. We will therefore see a global preference in retail banking and credit cards around 'customer empowerment'. This is because banks and credit cards understand that, while they are seldom the most popular brands, they help people achieve goals. 'Empowerment' or 'life facilitation' is a consumer goal. If you look at the top national banks in your country and consider their positioning, I bet 'life facilitation' drives the majority them!

As a further example, let's continue with our fictitious airlines. Each brand has a different core business focus. The core focus led to a category definition that naturally defines a broad but relevant customer base with multiple consumer category goals.

- **National Carrier consumer goals:** Our market prefers to fly a major, full-service airline. They enjoy the national affinity shared with the national airline carrier (if relevant). They want the level of service and convenience afforded to a major airline domestically and internationally – the wide choice and frequency of travel routes. On the ground, they want to travel to and from major airports. They prefer the preferential positioning for check-in and exclusive loyalty lounges. In the air, they enjoy an expected level of service befitting a major carrier.

- **Summarised consumer goals:** In this category, consumers fly major full-service airlines for the choice, convenience and comfort, but also for the internal self-worth and external status it affords.

The choice of a major airline is influenced by internal and external perceptual factors. People self-identify with their airline of choice. The airline they choose infers something about who they are and how they want to be perceived. The goal of a full-service airline domestically and internationally is to get you from A to B as conveniently and as comfortably as possible. The focus is around the journey and making it effortless, comfortable and enjoyable.

- **Budget Airline consumer goals:** Our market prefers to fly with low-fare airlines because it gives them the opportunity to explore and experience more domestic and international locations. They are not concerned with preferential treatment. They want the basics only with the value that brings. They are more concerned with the experience of the destination than the journey.
- **Summarised consumer goals:** Customers seeking fun, affordable and exciting experiences both domestically and internationally choose us for our reach into new and exotic destinations.

Consumers of discount airlines are less concerned with the range of destinations, the major airports on the route, flight times, the ability to choose a class, or the quality of the on-ground and in-air service. Discount, low-fare airlines have enabled them to travel to places previously out of reach. Or travel more regularly to more destinations. The focus is around the destination.

Following the techniques illustrated above will help develop a contextual understanding of the motivations and goals of the consumer in our category.

We should typically identify between two and four consumer category goals. If it seems there are too many, 'ladder' them up again and try to find the common consumer goal. A good way to check this section is by taking random popular brands within the category and seeing if they fit within the stated goals – if they don't, we need to do more work. Keep going until no brand does not fit into the consumer goals categories. Once this is accomplished, it is time to move to the next question and consider our brand strengths, or the Brand Assets.

Brand Assets

Brand Assets: What are the brand's strengths?		
Meaning:	**Process:**	**Outcome:**
Define our own brand attributes: product and service attributes and features. Identifying our own brand benefits: product and consumer benefits.	Unpack the product or service attributes. Where are we strongest? Search for distinct hooks and angles. Group attributes leading to product and consumer benefits.	A thorough investigation of all the potential existent brand attributes that appeal to consumer. A concise statement of the subsequent product and brand benefits.

Meaning

In the previous section, we focused on the consumer goal within the *category*. In this section we remain focused on the consumer, but now consider how our brand *benefits* the consumer. The natural flow of the Causality model is irresistible at this stage. Having focused on the category goals, we will immediately become focused around our own brand strengths that facilitate these goals. This is desired, but be careful to explore every aspect of the brand, not just those that support previous goals. (We do not want to miss an opportunity that the customer has not yet recognised as a goal, which might be achievable through our brand assets). We will answer this question by bringing the Consumer Goal and the Brand Assets questions together in the final Core Concept: The Brand's Truth.

A Brand Asset (within the Brand Causality model) is arrived at through defining, firstly, the *brand attributes* and secondly, the subsequent *brand benefits*. A brand attribute is its product/service attributes and features – an actual tangible component of the brand and/or a strength or skill that our brand utilises to create appeal for the customer. Once those attributes are determined, we progress to the second part of the question, to consider our own *brand benefits*. A brand benefit is the resulting product or consumer value resulting from the attributes.

Process

We are not asking for competitive uniqueness (or old-fashioned Unique Selling Propositions), which by definition are singular. We are looking for a number of brand aspects that include appealing attributes and benefits to the customer.

In today's modern market, competitive differentiation is hard to come by. I have only worked on a handful of brands that had a genuinely unique product or service attribute. Even if one exists, a brand should never be positioned solely around a specific attribute. What will that brand do when that feature (if successful) is ultimately adopted by the competition or the category?

The process is unsurprisingly sequential! We firstly look at the brand attributes (its product or service attributes and features). This ranges from a basic list of what we think we offer the consumer to an exhaustive investigation into product and service aspects. Product or service attributes can come from anywhere – a specific formulation or an aspect of service. Do not be afraid to get into the detail.

> I have always found it useful to conduct factory tours and talk in-depth with technical or product/service staff before projects or workshops. Advanced knowledge of the product or service is critical here. You either should know it yourself or have access to someone who does.

We have touched on product attributes or service features previously. But we do so now from our own brand (not category) point of view. How is our product and service distinct? How is it made, where is it made, who is it made by, how long does it last? How is the service run, what is the training, are there delivery guarantees or customer charters?

We need to determine all aspects of our brand that make it appealing to the consumer. We need to interrogate our own brand attributes and/or services ruthlessly! Once satisfied, take a step back and figuratively squint at the page. You will always see attributes that can be grouped together that will inspire product or consumer benefits.

You will now be able to move forward to the second stage and group brand attributes together to identify brand benefits (product and consumer benefits). Here we are utilising the laddering technique once more but applied to our brand. By way of reminder, the laddering technique takes a number of product or service attributes, groups them, then asks what the product benefit is. We then take the product benefit and ask what the consumer benefit might be (illustrated previously in the toothpaste examples). For further example:

The Car Market:

- Brand Attribute - 4x4 and Two-Wheel Drive
- Brand Product Benefit - Go anywhere
- Brand Consumer Benefit - Freedom

The Large Food Retail Market:

- Brand Attribute – Stocks unknown/secondary brands
- Brand Product Benefit – Lower prices
- Brand Consumer Benefit – Value

In utilising this technique within this section of the Brand Causality model, we are looking for the brand attributes and benefits *relevant to the product/service*. This is not a hypothetical exercise; there needs to be tangible evidence of these attributes and benefits from our brand. Let's consider the previous banking examples to illustrate, looking at how the attributes ramp up to the benefits in each case.

- **National Bank brand attributes:** We have multiple branches and ATMs, as well as 24-hours online and mobile banking services. We have multiple products including accounts, mortgages, credit cards and personal loans for consumers and much more for business banking. We have over 100 years' experience in providing financial services. We provide personal bankers when and where you need them.
- **National Bank brand benefits:** We have an easily accessible, extensive product range. With the experience and expertise to advise you when and where you need it.
- **Digital Bank brand attributes:** We provide the banking essentials, with low-cost fees, products are available 24/7, advice across all digital and social platforms.
- **Digital Bank brand benefits:** We are flexible, active and customer orientated. We offer a new and different choice within the market.

Even in the most commoditised and mature markets, there will be multiple 'hooks' or 'angles' that will identify themselves as brand attributes, which will in turn inform brand benefits.

Outcome

The right answers here are very much dependent on the brand in question. My advice is to always unpack the brand attributes as much as possible. This has a dual positive effect. If we claim 'customer service' as a brand strength, it obviously needs to be unpacked. What precisely about our customer service is a strength? We often learn more in this explanation, which gives rise to further strengths (e.g. We have a great call centre). Or we realise it is not a strength and should be abandoned (or at least a note made for the business to focus on the issue!).

Brand attributes (and their subsequent benefits) should be realistic and universally agreed upon. However, there are examples, especially when we have changed the Brand's Business or identified a Consumer Goal that wasn't previously the business focus, where they could be desired rather than existent. Desired brand strengths are permissible, but they must be already be in some way evident within the business. Even when evolving the Brand's Business, as brand transformation is desired, there will be existent attributes to focus on or build. This is also true when completing the Consumer Goals. Rarely do we find no existent attributes in the business, as the business would have naturally evolved based on category consumer demand. Hence, seldom are their no attributes that fit the evolved brand due to the sequential nature of the Brand Causality model. The process of selecting key attributes and focusing the power of the business on them is incredibly important for brand and business success.

By focusing on brand attributes that are appealing to your customer, you only develop 2-4 brand benefits. In terms of expression, we are led by sacrifice, brevity and causality. Hence, we start by listing the key brand attributes. The attributes are the building blocks for the benefits. In terms of expression, we include all the attributes in our workings. As stated already, isolating these is critical to the business in terms of focus and prioritisation.

But in the actual expression of the summary of the Brand Causality Model, we focus on the brand benefits. This is the key consumer section within the Causality model, and it is the consumer we seek to influence. Therefore, the critical information we include in our summaries in this section are the product and consumer benefits.

Continuing with our fictitious airline brands.

- **National Carrier brand attributes:** We developed air travel in this nation. We are a full-service airline, focused on high standards in lounges, seats, service, food and entertainment. We have a wide choice and frequency of travel times to and from national and international key airports.
- **Summarised brand benefits:** We are part of the nation's history, providing the highest domestic and international standards focused on customer service and care.
- **Budget Airline brand attributes:** We provide the lowest fares by keeping our overheads and costs to an absolute minimum. We offer a basic service, with friendly cabin crew, with extra services at an additional cost. We travel to major destinations and holiday spots.
- **Summarised brand benefits:** We are a great value airline, providing a variety of low-cost fares to favourite locations around the world, making air travel more accessible for all.

The Brand's Truth

The Brand's Truth: How we help the consumer achieve their goal		
Meaning: The reason why our brand helps them achieve their goal. Saliency is a greater goal than uniqueness. We work from the consumer to our brand, not from our brand to the consumer.	**Process:** Consider the key consumer goal(s) for the brand (considering brand assets). Consider the brand benefits and articulate how we help achieve their goal.	**Outcome:** Express the truth about the brand, from the brand's point of view. Inspired by the understanding of the consumer goal.

Meaning

The approach to this Core Concept is critical to the overall Brand Story and Essence. It is a question that is (or should be) asked at every level within a business. The Brand's Truth is what makes the brand salient to the consumer. We consider the identified consumer goals and brand assets and select a key consumer goal and supporting brand assets.

It is also an approach that deviates from the traditional brand positioning framework. This question within a traditional guide is usually concerned with a 'brand uniqueness' of some nature – why the brand should be selected by the consumer over the competition. Brand uniqueness typically and historically comes from the product or service itself.

Within this guide and framework, our approach is slightly, but, importantly, different. As you have seen, we focus first on the category and understand the broader motivation – the consumer goals within the category. We then ask for the definition of the Brand's Assets (the product and consumer benefits of the brand).

The difference comes in the 'definition of terms' in the Core Concept: The Brand's Truth. In this concept, we ask, 'How can we help the consumer achieve their goal?' Not, 'What is our product or service uniqueness?' A subtle difference, but one designed to force a consumer-focused brand approach versus a product or service-led brand approach.

The benefit of this method over the traditional is based on practical consumer understanding. It is a modern and realistic application in that it presupposes that the consumer is at least indifferent, and usually resistant to brand messaging. This is a much bigger topic – but suffice to say, the consumer is not an eager and willing recipient of most the world's brand messaging.

Hence, we need to understand and identify their broad category motivation and develop our Brand's Truth around the key relevant consumer goal(s) within that existent category. We can then identify Brand's Assets and develop a Brand Truth that is based on the relevant (not unique) brand assets that help achieve the relevant category consumer goals.

The question of uniqueness is not as critical to that of saliency. It is more important for a brand to be salient than it is for a brand to be 'different'. Why then do the tools of brand positioning (and communication for that matter) focus on uniqueness? We are asking the wrong question! If Apple owns 'creativity', and Coca-Cola 'happiness', these are not unique within their own categories. But they are relevant to their consumer's goals, and as brands, they associate themselves strongly with these themes (often making them seem unique).

Applying this, we should work from the consumer to our brand, not, as traditionally done, work from our brand to the consumer.

Process

At the risk of over-simplification, we have a list of a few consumer goals and a list of brand assets. Therefore, it will be evident, without too much consideration, what our consumer goal and supporting brand benefits will be. In some sessions, the brand benefits point clearly to a consumer goal. In other sessions, a favoured consumer goal allows us to pick and choose from several brand assets. The direction of analysis is less important than the outcome.

However, for direction, and given the philosophy of the 'consumer-over-product/service approach', we should always start with finalising the desired key consumer goal first. The sequential nature again leads us to a simple conclusion. By simply completing the process of consumer goals first, we will be unconsciously led to the brand benefit that supports these goals. In this way, the Brand's Truth is often written before we start!

If it feels that none of the brand assets match our chosen consumer goal, don't worry. This is not a scientific formula, it's a guide. Use common sense to manipulate, re-frame or evolve brand assets. But only within reason, if you genuinely have no current or latent assets that help a consumer goal, you will have to look at your product or service offering again.

On a theoretical level, we will naturally gravitate our brand and business to a consumer (over product) approach. We will be helping to fulfill a consumer goal rather than selling a product.

A favoured saying of 'trust the process' is prevalent in our industry, and it is true here. If we allow ourselves to defend previous thinking or preconceived ideas of what the Brand's Truth should be, this section will be difficult as we try to force-fit our answer. If, on the other hand, we abandon ourselves to the process, we will find one of the most challenging questions to answer within brand positioning self-evident.

At a superficial level, it is a matching process that works both ways. As a group or an individual, we should consider our key consumer goals against our brand benefits and develop the Brand's Truth.

At a deeper level, we must make some sacrifices. We will have to choose the most relevant consumer goal, with the knowledge of our brand assets. This will mean abandoning other goals and assets. Alternatively, we can work to 'ladder' the goals and assets to a point where they encompass multiple answers. The ramifications for our brand are considerable. Therefore, the choices we make here are critical.

Outcome

So how do we make sure we choose the right one? The simple answer is to go with what feels right. While this instruction is not necessarily the most illustrative to the reader, take solace in the fact that experience proves this to be correct. Each session, or when working through session notes by myself, a consumer goal will always stand out and will make sense. It will provoke the 'of course that's it' reaction discussed earlier.

The process behind this Core Concept, the Formative Questions, have been designed to lead us to the right answer, or at least provide us with the building blocks or options for the right answer.

The first Formative Question, Consumer Goals, forces consideration of the category; you will have defined key consumer goals within that category. You will be looking at the world through the eyes of a consumer. You will have a broad view of what, beyond the functional, are their needs. These should vary. Within every category, there are a variety of needs that current brands meet or need to be met. Identification of different or similar (core driving) consumer category needs, gives the context to find the Brand's Truth for our brand.

The second Formative Question, Brand Assets, gives you the direction you need, guiding you towards the specific consumer goal your brand is best suited, or desired, to answer. The process is always interesting, often liberating. It allows you to look up and reconnect with the market and consumer reality.

In terms of expression, the Brand's Truth should be written in a concise, single-minded way. No interpretation, or double meaning, is acceptable. As always, clear not clever.

We need to articulate a truth about the brand. A truth that is born from our understanding of the consumer goal that is most appealing to our customer and fits our brand attributes and benefits.

We can and should make a leap (in most cases); however, we could have already articulated the brand truth in the previous Brand Truth sections. As you will see from the examples the right answer is the one that is most congruent. We know what our category consumer wants, we have aligned our assets and expressed them as a benefit to the customer. Within our Brand's Truth we articulate the truth of our brand – the reason why we help them achieve their goal.

Let's reconsider our bank brands with our more detailed knowledge. To demonstrate the 'flow', we'll look at Consumer Goal, Brand Asset and then Brand Truth in each example.

National Bank

- **Consumer Goal:** Bank with trust, simplicity, familiarity and specialist expertise.
- **Brand Assets:** We have an easily accessible, extensive product range. With the experience and expertise to advise you when and where you need it.
- **The Brand's Truth:** When you need us most in life, we will be there to offer the right advice.

Digital Bank

- **Consumer Goal:** A new way of banking, with tailored products and seamless delivery.
- **Brand Assets:** We are flexible, active and customer orientated. We offer a new and different choice within the market.

- **The Brand's Truth:** We provide a new, straightforward and better value approach to banking.

Let's now consider our airline examples to illustrate how you might express the Brand's Truth. Remember these are examples – it is a quasi-creative process, so treat the examples as an illustration of my style (everyone's is different!). What could be the Brand Truths for our airlines?

- **National Carrier Brand's Truth:** A superior customer experience in air travel.
- **Budget Airline Brand's Truth:** Helping more people enjoy and experience popular destinations through accessible air travel.

One last note on expression before we move to the next Core Concept. As always, I encourage the reader to find their own expression. But when familiarising with the Brand Causality model, I know instruction around expression helps understanding. I therefore express the truth about the brand, from the brand's point of view, inspired by the understanding of the consumer goal. Within this Core Concept you need to articulate what your brand does for your consumer.

4

Core Concept 3: The Brand's Spirit

Belief System

Belief System: What cultural beliefs drive the brand?		
Meaning: To define the key aspects of the internal culture and the internal cultural beliefs that drive the brand.	**Process:** Identify original beliefs within the business. Understand current aspects of dominant culture. Use The Brand's Truth to evolve or fit new cultures.	**Outcome:** Not a list of adjectives. Must inspire and engender pride. Are an organic 'system' interconnected and dependent on each other.

Meaning

In this question, we are seeking to define key aspects of the internal culture that has brought the brand to this point. Here, we again differ from a [or the] traditional brand positioning process. Hence, a further (simple) explanation is required. Within typical theory, most approaches seek to immediately find brand values that are consistent with the brand and, in most cases, the company behind the brand, arguing – quite rightly – that a brand and company must have consistent values. A company cannot be traditional and conservative and launch or define an anti-establishment brand – it would fail.

There are exceptions to this rule found within large and/or multi-national companies who operate a 'house of brands' architecture. This term is used for a company that operates in the background, preferring to build and 'hero' its brands. The most notable example is Unilever and Procter & Gamble – this is how Axe/Lynx and Dove can (albeit increasingly less comfortably) come from the same company, Unilever. In these cases, the focus is on the brand's, not the company's, values. Hence the brand strategy mirrors the brand architectural approach.

In most cases, the beliefs of the brand must be consistent with the company. However, to presume they should be the same does not allow sufficient exploration of these two critical elements: the brand's internal culture and the brand's external perception.

We split out these questions within our process, unifying them within the conclusion: the Brand's Spirit. The Brand's Spirit is critical to the perception of the brand. What people feel toward the brand is generated by the internal ethos as much as the brand's external perception. It is, therefore, essential to devise a framework (this model), that allows analysis of internal (belief system) and external (brand feeling) to formulate the Brand's Spirit.

Suppose we are not happy with where we are or have redefined the Brand's Business. In that case, we must look to evolve, or more rarely, create completely new aspects of culture. As stated, brands seldom need complete change. Evolution or reframing them internally is often preferable. Hence, it is always worth considering the actual cultural values.

The purposeful use of a belief system over the more traditional cultural values is not wordplay, but a declaration of intent, as is the title of this critical Core Concept: The Brand's Spirit.

Like a Brand's Spirit, a belief system is explicit in seeking to define something more than a list of cultural adjectives, usually, 'Innovative', 'Down to Earth' or 'Progressive' (recognise any?). In my experience, the business behind the brand has weaknesses and failings, but also has *a living breathing sense of self* – often unwritten ways of working and internal ethics, values or credos. It is these elements we need to capture and articulate.

Brands are like people, and as people, they can be described with internal belief systems (that manifest externally as character). In this Formative Question, we are concerned with the inner belief system. It is, therefore, to be considered from an internal brand and business point of view. We are turning the focus, momentarily, back inside the brand. What is it that defines and drives the inner beliefs of the brand and business? We do this perhaps with an altered focus, in that we now have a defined Brand Truth. The process will guide us – consider this question within the new, evolved or at least a clearly defined context.

Process

In answering this question, as always, a staged and sequential approach will help. As discussed, it will also depend on what we have previously decided as to what techniques we apply.

Initially, looking to the past is the best starting point. We should remind ourselves here of the very first Formative Question asked: Why was this brand created? Within these answers, we may find some fundamental internal cultural beliefs (often found around the creator's personal beliefs that have become 'systemised' within the brand, like Virgin).

Brands are made over time; the time frame can be dramatically different, but nonetheless they evolve. In that initial evolution, there will be aspects of an internal culture that have been more dominant than others. What are they? Often many brands have defining moments where they 'change course' or 'refocus' – what are the beliefs behind that change?

Having considered the above, it's time to move on to consider current day business – what are the cultural beliefs driving the business? It can be cathartic to order these from negative to positive. It is often interesting how people's experience, and therefore views of these beliefs, can place the same belief as a positive and a negative. The ensuing discussion will always be useful and will decide, if at all, where the belief features.

Finally, having worked through the past and present, it's time to consider the future – but considering it in terms of the previously defined Brand's Truth. The Brand's Truth gives us internal direction, what beliefs we need to focus on to support the Brand Truth. The language, tone and message within the Brand's Truth will give us clues on where to focus, in terms of our internal beliefs.

Outcome

The right answer should not look like a list of adjectives. Traditional cultural values are not only uninspiring but dangerous and open to interpretation. Luckily, if these exist within an organisation, they are so all-encompassing and lacking in personal resonance that they are often forgotten.

Expression is key within all aspects of brand strategy, but is incredibly important here, or at least worth spending more time on its impact. By now, my frustration with 'big words' within this traditional area of brand positioning strategy has become apparent. But the blame lies mostly with those that help develop them more than with the brand owners themselves.

In terms of practical guidance, when developing cultural beliefs that will drive a business and the Brand's Spirit – they must have an immediate and emotional impact. We are not all copywriters, but we are all people! We know if something moves us, makes us feel proud as well as being ownable and demonstrable. The driving beliefs must make us feel proud; they must have the power to inspire.

In this sense, they must be expressed in a way that facilitates the desired emotional reaction. I am reminded of an example from my (sadly lost – never loan your books out!) little blue book of *How to Plan Advertising* by Damian O'Malley (AGP, 1987). The example was for writing an advertising brief, but I am bending it to my purpose. Imagine we were writing the brief for Michelangelo when painting the Sistine Chapel:

We could have phrased it in various ways:

- Please paint the ceiling.
- Please paint the ceiling using red, green and yellow paint.
- We've got terrible problems with cracks in the ceiling. Can you cover it up for us?

Here was the actual brief Michelangelo was given:

- Please paint our ceiling for the greater glory of God and as an inspiration and lesson to his people.

The impact of the words matters. In defining the brand's beliefs, we are not just articulating a set of internal ideas for the brand, but a belief system for all the people who within our business encounter and curate the brand.

Lastly, the word 'system' is critical. Understanding brands as interconnected organic systems is a little strange but useful. The premise extends to how what one part does impacts all other aspects – an obvious theoretical concept.

Hence, the definitions here must be interrelated or connected – again, no white rabbits! If we articulate quite progressive beliefs, we can't slip in traditional or conservative words. Remember, we are defining the core beliefs; they should be all-encompassing, but we need not state the obvious. They must also be realistic, accurate and true. If future based, they should be based on realistic and achievable aspects of the existing platform. They should become the benchmark for internal operations across our business. The minute we give up on one of them, in any part on the business, they are all useless.

One more time for emphasis: The minute we give up on one of them, in any part on the business – they are all useless!

Let's look at our fictitious banks for example.

- **National Bank:** We believe in responsibility, understanding and expertise. Beliefs that guide us through the good and bad, boom and bust of our customers' lives and our nation's history.
- **Digital Bank:** We believe in better, an agile and transparent approach. We are a digital innovator forging a new way forward in financial service products and service.

For further example, our airline belief systems:

- **National Carrier belief system:** We are proud of our heritage and representation of the nation. We built the aviation industry in this country, helping the nation come together, grow and discover the world. We never cease improving our service, through new planes and new technology and infrastructure that makes the entire customer experience better. Our love for the magic of flying and the pleasure in bringing that to our customers remains. We want to make every journey easier, more comfortable and enjoyable.
- **Summarised belief system:** We believe in the magic of flying. We are a proud in creating the best experience for our customers every time they fly.
- **Budget Airline belief system:** We do not have, nor have ever had, the advantage of heritage. We entered a market that was

dominated by global brands with rich histories. We fought tooth and nail to initially survive and then thrive. Driven by the principle of low cost, we are continually looking for more efficiencies within our business and to keep our costs low so we can maintain the lowest priced fares for our customers. We are continually evolving and questioning where we will go next, we have no sacred cows and enjoy and thrive on change and challenge.

- **Summarised belief system:** We believe in fair; we thrive on change and challenge. We reject tradition and privilege, we are driven by getting the best value price in every aspect of our business, every day.

You will note that I like to start the summary of the belief system with 'we believe'. This is a stylistic choice; I find it helps to guide the following content into cultural values. It ensures we focus on the internal drivers of the brand, giving clear differentiation from the following section, which focuses on the external properties of our brand.

Brand Feeling

Brand Feeling: What are the brand's purpose and character?		
Meaning: How we want our consumer to view our brand. We articulate two interrelated aspects – the brand's societal or cultural purpose and its character.	**Process:** What is the brand's role in society? Develop associated human characteristics that will influence and shape brand perception.	**Outcome:** An aspirational societal brand goal that engenders pride and passion. A brand character, creating a clear, expressive picture of the brand persona.

Meaning

The brand feeling is how we want our consumer to view our brand. We articulate the feeling by considering two interrelated aspects – the brand's purpose and character. Within the previous question, we considered the internal belief system. Within this question, we consider the external consumer view of the brand. The consumer view is a perception made up of what they believe the brand stands for and the associations they attribute to the brand. These questions should, therefore, be determined from a consumer viewpoint. What do we want to communicate about our brand to the consumer? What do we want them to think and feel about our brand?

The purpose of a brand is defined here as a societal or cultural purpose. Close, but different from a more traditional 'vision'. Often visions are defined as where the company wants to be (and the 'mission' is how it gets there). The terms vision and mission are, to my mind, a little dated and internally focused. Through the course of this process, there are internal focus points, times when we are driven by the business over the customer. But in this Formative Question, we are seeking our higher-order purpose to the consumer and their society or culture. We are answering the question: What is the ultimate idea of our brand to our consumer's society or culture? What is the brand's societal purpose? This should not be confused with a benefit. Previously we have examined benefits within the Brand Truth Core Concept. We examined the benefits of the relevant category, and we examined the product and consumer benefits of our brand. We have not yet examined the benefit of the brand at a societal or cultural level.

The second element is the 'character' of the brand. Like its purpose, which demands something more consumer-based than business-focused, the choice of the word 'character' is all-encompassing and free from technicalities.

We are concerned here with the character elements of our brand that will influence what our consumers think and feel. These elements and the associations they create can come in any form; they're not limited to profiles, personality traits or attitudes, but a mixture of them. It is the human characteristics that we want people to associate with our brand: a critical shortcut to how a customer describes our brand and the connection they have with it. In this part of the Formative Question, we are trying to build the key characteristics that we want our consumer to attribute to our brand.

Process

Defining our brand's purpose immediately takes us away from business visions. It forces us to consider what is the brand's role in society and culture for our consumer.

For some, a big thought. We might argue that running a local café versus, for example, McDonald's, would have less impact on the world – and obviously, you do. But in terms of brand success (on a relative scale), the café still needs a purpose to be successful. No matter the size of a brand, it must have a higher goal beyond profit.

Techniques used here are asking yourself or the group: If the brand died, what might be written in its obituary? What were its most significant achievements for the consumer within society? We can also ask, if the brand was protesting for or against something, what might the placards read? Similarly, if the brand was to make the front page of a newspaper (try a local and national example) – what would the headline read?

Challenger or disruptive brand theory (Morgan and Dru) can also be very useful and applied at this stage. These and other brand positioning frameworks also look at questions to identify 'enemies' of the brand.

We can utilise these principles here to help us develop our brand purpose. Often a brand can define its role by finding and identifying its nemesis. The nemesis can take any form as long as it is big! For as any writer knows, the hero's tenacity and courage is directly proportional to the enemy's depth and scale of malice. Therefore, what are we fighting against on behalf of our consumer? What endemic social wrong do we want to put right?

Defining our brand's character seeks to identify and project certain human aspects that will influence and shape your brand in public.

Anyone who has sat through a focus group defining brand perceptions will be familiar with the projective techniques used as a researcher: 'Imagine brand X was a person. Who are they (gender, age); where would they live, work; what would they do in their spare time; what attitudes or characteristics does this person have?' etc. Utilising this technique over the years has given brand owners incredible insight into how the consumer has positioned their brand (and that of their competitors) in their own personal brand universe.

Similarly, in brand workshops all over the world, I have asked clients to describe brands, separating the response into two columns (without naming them). Then, when complete, they title one column 'rational' (this usually includes design, range and product features) the other 'emotional'. The emotional column always contains more words, and those words are human characteristics. The conclusions to this quasi-experiment are far-reaching but straightforward.

Brands are differentiated mainly within a framework of human characteristics.

Within consumer groups, you 'force' the personalisation – making consumers answer as if the brand has walked into the room in human form. Still, I suspect (from experience) that even without the 'forced projective technique', consumers would answer along the same lines as brand owners: primarily through defining human characteristics.

Like most observations, this is common sense. We utilise a framework we are familiar with when asked to describe something, so we default to the way we describe people. But understanding this puts enormous importance on defining or influencing the brand's character.

Many of the world's most successful brands work hard on establishing and maintaining a brand perception or feeling in the eyes of their customers. But too often, this side of brand positioning is not given the time and gravitas it deserves. We must embrace the more empathetic and emotional side of brand positioning. We cannot leave it unwritten or, worse, define usual uninspiring perception.

There are many approaches to defining the brand character. It is, of course, useful in workshops or alone to be guided by gut or spontaneous reaction. Most commonly, as described above, we need to transform our brand into a person. The first and often illuminating questions we can ask ourselves is what gender and age the brand is, then consider defining attitudes and personality traits. A rule of thumb here, based on saliency, is if your brand is younger or older than your core category target, something might be wrong.

Some people and groups find this easy; others are resistant. I suspect the variation has more to do with the personality of the respondent rather than the brand in question. Regardless, sometimes we must work hard to get to an answer, sometimes it comes naturally. Asking the same question in different ways can be helpful. It can, therefore, be useful to compare ourselves to the leading or closest competitor. Sometimes we find it easier to define our brand character in opposition to another (remember the 'defining' Apple versus PC television commercials).

However, other techniques differ from human characterisation. Exploring the brand through the five senses is an interesting approach, 'When you consider our brand – what do you see, smell, hear, taste and touch?' Another technique, which I have used frequently (and recently seen referenced in *Brand Seduction* by Daryl Weber [2016]), is the idea of 'brand planets'. I like the large scope of this idea, it gives enough breadth to explore everything: atmosphere, environment, architecture, language, society, as well as the populace, who are they, what do they look like, what do they believe, how do they act, etc. I was originally inspired to use this technique after reading *Men are from Mars, Women are from Venus* by John Gray (1992). This highlights the creative concept for understanding how the difference between men and women is that they were originally from different planets! These planets had different social structures, attitudes, values and expected personality traits. Hence, it is a useful creative platform to understand and define your brand character.

What might planet Apple look like versus planet IBM? Or, more challenging but as interesting, what might planet Pepsi look like versus planet Coca-Cola? This technique can be used in isolation, but it does come to life in comparison. Importantly, when analysing the findings in this process, bring them back to human brand characteristics. Don't discard or ignore the other non-human findings, just interpret them in a way to bring you back to human characterisation.

There are several practical considerations in answering this question. We don't need to be too technical or concerned with classification here. It doesn't matter what comes to mind; it just matters that it comes to mind. So, brainstorm or collect all the responses to the initial question in a group – If our brand were a person, what characteristics would they have? People answer this question with demographic, personality, attitude and value responses. There is no wrong answer.

Also, we need to beware of self-projection. Often individuals and particularly brand teams can project their own personal desired or aspirational characteristics into their brand. This can be useful, but the brand should outlast the team! We need to spend time considering contrasting characteristics. It is not uncommon for a team to disagree on certain aspects of character. We must mediate to a common shared answer.

Finally, and without apology, we need to trust in the process! We will have defined or evolved aspects of our brand up to this point. We must consider the impact on these definitions on our brand's character. If we have significantly evolved the brand, we can't 'throw the baby out with the bathwater'. There will always be character aspects that have defined the brand in the past that we can bring forward into the desired future. We need to be comfortable with them within the new context.

This is a strategic process with far-reaching impacts on the practical running of a business. Decisions you make here should impact every touchpoint with the consumer. If you change, evolve or refresh the brand's character, it must ultimately be reflected in the business – the product and service offering and experience, brand identity, website and marketing, through to recruitment and workspace environment.

The brand character must be considered with an understanding of its successful implementation. Do not be glib or treat this process as the 'fun part'. It is usually much more important than anyone thinks.

Outcome

The reason this Core Concept comes later in the process is that we need the previous context to inform our answer. We should be looking for 'cognitive ease' – the flow of one concept to another, or one answer inspiring the next.

This question is designed to free us from the usual business-focused aims (we want to be number one) and elevate the conversation to how we help society achieve a broad and worthwhile goal or how we positively influence culture. It should feel big; it should make us proud. This is the ultimate 'rule of thumb' for our brand purpose. When we read it back or out loud, it should trigger a positive emotional reaction. I have seen this question galvanise brands through the creation of a common enemy or a shared positive purpose. It can focus, refresh or evolve a brand, giving it new energy and enthusiasm.

The difference between a 'brand purpose' and a 'brand vision' is important to consider before we look at some examples. It is possible to use some of the better iconic brand visions as illustration and inspiration for great brand purposes. However, not all brand visions can be used. Here, again, the carefully selected wording gives us direction. In too many cases (in my opinion), iconic brands miss the mark with 'brand visions' focused on themselves instead of what they do for their customer. Words and phrasing are critical in brand strategy, as is the consultant's definition of them, if one is leading you through the process. A brand vision all too often becomes business, not consumer, focused. You can become too fixed on what you want the company to be, rather than what ultimate goal it plays in society for the customer. We use the word 'purpose' for this reason. It is a reminder that, while here to turn a profit, a successful brand will come from helping the society achieve a high-level goal. This is not to be confused with corporate social responsibility. The clue's in the title! A corporation's role supporting charities and the communities they operate within should not be confused with the brand's purpose, although a good Brand Purpose will give direction to corporate responsibility.

My favourite example for inspiration (they are subject to change by brand owners) is Apple (sorry):

'To make a contribution to the world by making tools for the mind that advance humankind.'

Although it might never have been Apple's actual vision or mission statement (hence the urban myth grown around it), it is still a powerful illustration of the 'level' of purpose we should aspire to.

It is a single, short expression of the brand's societal goal on behalf of the consumer. This, what I would term 'brand purpose', has been replaced with other turgid and corporate statements since, much to the concern and wrath of the Apple faithful.

There are, unfortunately, not many examples among the brands discussed so far. We need to look further afield for brand purpose examples. IDEO is a company that understands brand purpose. Reflected in their work for The North Face, on their US website they define (in part) The North Face purpose as:

'We exist to encourage exploration'.

(IDEO US website US/ blog / retrieved July 2020, retrieved from https://www.ideo.com/blog/design-an-organizations-purpose-statement-with-this-tool).

The IDEO strategy of considering the reason for the brand's existence is a useful technique in defining a brand purpose. As we have discussed, both Apple and The North Face have identified their own reason for existing for their customer.

For further illustration, let's refer back to our initial banking examples.

- **National Bank's brand purpose:** We are going back to the heart of banking: helping people, families and communities reach their fullest potential.

- **Digital Bank's brand purpose:** We want to change the nature of daily banking and embrace positive customer engagement.

Getting to the right character is an exercise in creative and strategic thinking. Practically, there are a limited number of adjectives that are used to describe people. It is, therefore, not unusual that here (as in belief systems) you get the re-occurrence of 'the usual suspect' traits that are often used by the business to describe the brand. It is important to reject these from the outset because they have (mostly) already become meaningless; or, if they really do work, find new ways to express them.

By this stage in the process, we have declared our core internal beliefs, which by their nature tend to be more conservative. Having identified these, we find ourselves free to explore more exciting and creative character traits. We should have also crafted a brand purpose that makes us proud. This will lead us into a funnel or filter and helps identify the aspects of character that are most pertinent to the purpose.

The right language is important in expressing our beliefs (i.e. the Sistine Chapel example). Hence, unpacking the language is critical, and looking for expressive ways to communicate the character is vital. Consider the word 'fresh'. Strategically it can mean promiscuous, clean, new, bright or young – an expressive word, but multi-dimensional. Big strategic terms require a very detailed explanation of precisely what is meant by them and are often better broken down.

The number of aspects required for a brand character should be few – not too few to be generic and too many to be confusing (or a compromise for opposing opinions). The best advice I can give is to keep digging into the brand's character to ensure a clear insight and idea of who this brand is and why. Ultimately (and this is a good test) pick random human scenarios that test character, for example speeches, deaths, conflict, presentations, or other dilemmas, and determine how the brand would respond. If we can confidently predict and describe our brand's response, we have defined the character well. If we are doubtful or mixed in our responses, we have more work to complete.

For example, our airlines' purpose and character:

- **National Carrier purpose:** To continually improve and redefine the expected level of customer service in air travel.
- **National Carrier character:** We mirror the service you receive in the best hotels and restaurants: expert and professional, always open, courteous and thoughtful. We pride ourselves on anticipating and catering to all our customers' needs throughout their journey with us.
- **Budget Airline purpose:** To fight hard for discounted air travel, so everyone has access to the freedom and adventure that travel brings.
- **Budget Airline character:** Youthful, informal, irrepressible and inventive; we were born for adventure.

The Brand's Spirit

The Brand's Spirit: Cultural and consumer social guidelines		
Meaning:	**Process:**	**Outcome:**
To create a societal purpose or cultural relevance for the brand. Defining a set of social guidelines for the brand to live by.	Previous evaluation is different to final expression. Take the purpose and evolve supporting elements from beliefs and character.	A narrative explaining the higher goal of the brand. Supported and expressed in: purpose, beliefs and personality.

Meaning

When defining this Core Concept, we are ultimately preparing a set of social guidelines for our brand. A manifesto, or credo that determines its beliefs, purpose and character.

The order of the Formative Questions is by design, forcing certain points of view as we progress to ensure full internal and external investigation. In answering the final Core Concept, we determine the key aspect from the cultural beliefs, the purpose and character into a narrative that encapsulates the Brand's Spirit.

At this stage, we are answering from a brand point of view. What defines our Brand's Spirit? This is a question that relies (as always) on building one answer from the next. In constructing the answer to this Core Concept, there is some complexity, but for reasons of simplicity!

Process

The method of evaluation is different from the method of final expression. The method of evaluation, through the Formative Questions, asks to first look internally and identify key internal beliefs. Once identified, we define a single brand-consumer-societal purpose, then the associated human characteristics of the brand to support the purpose.

The method of expression, in crafting this Core Concept, is slightly different to the evaluative process. In expressing the Brand's Spirit, we first take the brand's purpose and then fit or evolve the supporting internal belief aspect(s) and key supporting aspect(s) of the brand's character.

The Brand's Spirit should ultimately be the same internally as externally. However, a process is required to make sure we are not constructing a brand character that does not fit with the internal culture.

Outcome

In terms of expression, this concept has been designed to help you construct the classic elements that make a brand's character. Explain the higher goal of the brand, and using the relevant internal beliefs and characteristics, build a sequential narrative. Applying common sense and creative thinking in the narrative, so it flows from one element to another, builds a clear and engaging sense of what the brand 'believes in' and wants to be perceived as.

This process seeks to guide to territories that help us make better brand decisions (it doesn't answer for us). This is especially true within this Core Concept. Any Brand's Spirit is always challenging to define well. It is also all too easy to skate on the surface and fail to deeply and properly define.

Ultimately, we should consider other brands. In writing about brands we love, it will become clear that they have clearly defined beliefs, purpose and character that we either identify with or respect. They stand for something and are consistent in communication and action of that stance.

I think the most challenging thing in modern business is to consistently portray a brand spirit through the entire brand experience. But defining it clearly and expressively is the first step on that difficult road; without it (and with so many contributing and competing voices), it will easily become confused and over time lost.

Let's consider our airline examples for illustration.

I hesitate with these examples here because while I am seeking to guide you through a process and give practical and useful insight to achieve the best answers, the expression within this section is subjective. And that's a good thing!

To this end let's recap our Formative Questions in this section. As you will note, brevity and simplicity are incredibly difficult but ultimately worthwhile. We will always have the (slightly) longer answers from the previous sections for clearer explanation. But with the Brand's Spirit, we must sacrifice more than anywhere else, and be ruthless. What is the expression that crystallises the Brand's Spirit?

National Carrier

- **Belief system:** We believe in the magic of flying and in creating the best experience for our customers every time they fly.
- **Purpose:** To continually improve and redefine the expected level of customer service in air travel.
- **Character:** We mirror the service you receive in the best hotels and restaurants: expert and professional, always open, courteous and thoughtful. We pride ourselves on anticipating and catering to all our customers' needs throughout their journey with us.
- **Brand's Spirit:** Dedicated to making each flight a magical experience.

Budget Airline

- **Belief system:** We are an irrepressible brand. We thrive on change and challenge. We are determined to bring low cost to as many people and destinations as we can.
- **Purpose:** To fight hard for discounted air travel, so everyone has access to the freedom and adventure that travel brings.
- **Character:** We are youthful, informal, irrepressible and inventive; we were born for adventure.
- **Brand's Spirit:** Giving adventure and freedom to as many people as we can.

Determining the spirit of a brand is challenging but very exciting. The tools and methods within Brand Causality will guide you to the answer. You can see how the Brand's Spirit captures the very nature of the brand. Our National Airline is 'dedicated to making each flight a magical experience'; something only a national airline like British Airways or Qantas could deliver. The spirit of the brand exudes class, luxury, premium service and ease. For our Budget Airline the spirit is very different, 'giving adventure and freedom to as many people as we can'. This brand spirit is 'for the people'; it is younger with much more energy and fight, personifying the brand benefits and creating distinction against the implied 'traditional and stuffy' competition.

5

Defining Concepts: The Brand Story and Brand Essence

The Brand Story

The Brand Story: The confluence of the core concepts in a story		
Meaning: The story of the brand. Utilising key points of interest and the Core Concepts into a short Brand Story.	**Process:** The concepts detail our core business and focus. How we help the consumer in our category with our assets. Our beliefs, purpose and character: ingredients for a great story.	**Outcome:** A seamless, engaging and simple Brand Story that defines our brand's positioning in the market and in the mind of the consumer.

Meaning

Congratulations – we have reached the end of the process!

The first Defining Concept is the Brand Story. The Brand Story is a 100-word story inspired by the answers to the Formative Questions and Core Concepts you have already completed. Over the years, I have evolved my thinking on the inclusion of this question, as mentioned in the introduction. This sequential process has been developed to lend itself to a brand summary or story.

People like stories – they always have. It is a fundamental part of our culture. It is, therefore, not an incredible leap that our brand should create and share its own story. There is a great benefit in being challenged to write the Brand Story. We don't truly understand a subject unless we write about it. Something magical happens in the process – the brand becomes something more than it was. Many writers have talked about stories taking on a life of their own!

Process

The Brand Causality model itself is the guide to creating the Brand Story. The Formative Questions make the Core Concepts, and the Core Concepts make the Brand Story. Typically, the Core Concepts will dominate the story of your brand. As they should – 100 words as you will find out, is not a lot! You have to be very focused on the key elements you want to include. However, this is not as simple as writing down the Core Concepts; you need to create a flow, an inarguable dialogue that naturally results in the Brand Essence. Much of the work has been completed, as the Core Concepts are designed to concisely define and position our brand. We have defined the business we are in, what our consumer wants from the category and how our product or service facilitates this. We have defined our internal culture and our societal goal for the consumer and what kind of brand we need to be to deliver that societal/cultural goal. We therefore naturally have all the ingredients of a very good story!

Be led by the core concepts but allow words and ideas from the answers to the Formative Questions to pervade your story. We just need to be careful not to 'overload' the story and create any 'white rabbit' points for this section.

Finally, remember this section is a summary into the Brand Story, so be guided by the work we have completed to date. It should also inspire us towards the final goal – the Brand Essence. When I am writing or thinking about a Brand Story is often when I get that flash of inspiration about what the Brand's Essence could be, so be ready!

Outcome

My practical advice is to start writing. Many have self-doubt at this stage, but it may be surprising. With the initial inspiration captured, we need to go through the Brand Story and cut it down to the bare bones. Believe me, I know how difficult this is! Once we've created a story, to which we have grown quite attached, the hardest thing is to cut it back to the engaging essentials. I often explain or read the initial Brand Story to my colleagues (verbally). During the different explanations, we find ourselves referring to the same points over and over and omitting others. This gives us a guide to what to cut and what to keep.

The final Brand Story should be 100 words (the length of this paragraph). I like the discipline of this; however, as always, this is a guide (although, try not to exceed 100 words). We are writing a story about our brand, its business focus, truth and its spirit. It should read fluently from one aspect to the next. It should be born from our previous work (Formative Questions and Core Concepts) but not a straight copy. We can utilise ideas and words from Core Concepts, but the challenge is to make them flow into a seamless, engaging, yet simple story.

By way of initial example let's look again at our banking examples:

- **National Bank:** We have grown with this nation, supporting the people who built it. Creating a broad range of products and services, easily available, to help achieve their financial goals whatever they are. Our broad experience and expertise mean we can guide our customers at times in their life when they need financial advice they trust. We want to get back to the heart of banking: to our customers, their families and communities. We will be human and open, using simple language, and will work hard to educate and be easily approachable. Making sure, when you need us most, we'll be there.

- **Digital Bank:** We are a contemporary approach to banking. We wanted to free ourselves from the traditional bricks and mortar and legacy products and attitudes of the old banks. We provide essential financial products across digital only platforms, supported with friendly customer support, which means lower fees and costs to our customers. A new straightforward, simple and better value approach to banking. We are creating a new concept in banking for a new breed of customers. We are unencumbered by the past and facilitated by modern attitudes and technology. We are changing banking for the better.

These illustrative examples show you the process described above. But they also show you the creative licence you have as the Brand Story author. Over 20 years of running and presenting different Brand Positioning outcomes, I have always been intrigued by the fact some brands 'lean into' certain Core Concepts. Our brand will lean into a certain concept, more than others. This often becomes evident when writing the Brand Story. It also gives you direction and inspiration for the final part of our process.

As a guide, let's write our airline Brand Stories.

- **National Carrier Brand Story:** We helped establish and evolve the aviation industry in this country to the high standards expected today. We have introduced new aircraft, technology and infrastructure that has seen our brand become recognised throughout our nation and the world as a premium, full-service airline. Our customers' experience is central to our successful development. We provide the highest domestic and international standards in customer service and care. However, we are always looking to improve and redefine this expected level of service. We pride ourselves on anticipating our customers' needs throughout their journey with us, making each and every flight magical.

- **Budget Airline Brand Story:** We fought hard to establish discount air travel into a market dominated by national carriers. We saw the opportunity to fly regular, low-cost flights to selected domestic and international destinations. We brought down the cost of air travel, making it fair, more accessible, helping people enjoy and experience popular destinations. People can now travel to places they have never been or travel more often. We have always challenged tradition. We are a youthful, informal and inventive brand born for adventure! We fight hard to provide low-cost, competitive flights so everyone can experience the sense of adventure and freedom travel brings.

The Brand Story begins to lead you to an inevitable conclusion. We find ourselves utilising all our breakthroughs, ideas, concepts and language in crafting the 100 words. We will invariably have a spark, a moment of inspiration, when a singular idea begins to formulate – this is when it is time to move to our conclusion and capture the single statement that defines our entire brand and the entire process!

The Brand Essence

The Brand Essence: A simple, familiar, emotionally engaging Idea		
Meaning:	**Process:**	**Outcome:**
The intrinsic nature or quality of the brand. The key defining element.	Identify key differentiating or recurrent themes using the Brand Story as inspiration.	A single concise idea. True to the product or service, distinct from the competition and engaging to the customer.

Meaning

We have considered many elements of the brand over time, through different points of view and strategic lenses, all of which we need to summarise into one single idea.

Firstly, having taught others, I would argue that brand positioning strategy, like creativity, can be learnt. Everyone is capable (given the right tools and training) of defining a brand's essence. Every exercise we have been through to get here has prepared us to answer this question. It should be no surprise by now that the discipline of positioning a brand, as in this guide, is an exercise in causality – asking simple questions whose answers inform concepts that in turn inform our brand's positioning. The coming together, the merging of multiple strands of information to specific points, then taking those points and merging them into an overall idea. Every question, concept or summary in this process asks us to do this. So, we should be more accustomed and comfortable with the exercise now than we were at the beginning of this process.

In fact, we should have the platform or territory for our Brand Essence already.

Process

We should have a few ideas of the nature and potential directions we could follow in this final step. The answer – the Brand Essence – often occurs in a repeated theme. Over the years, when working on a brand positioning or within a workshop, I have noticed how there is almost always a consistent theme or idea, evident or discussed, about the brand in question. This idea continually makes its way into the findings in multiple sections. This is sometimes the answer or, more likely, the platform from which to find the answer.

Consistency is essential in brands and the brand positioning process. It would not, therefore, be surprising that the convergent process remains. We use the Formative Questions to inform the Core Concepts; the Core Concepts to inform the Brand Story, and the Brand Story is the inspiration for the Brand Essence.

Outcome

The essence of a brand needs to be simple. It needs to be easily understandable – no play on words or dual concepts. It needs to be something a grandmother or a child would understand. 'If you can't explain it to a six-year-old, you don't understand it yourself' (Einstein). Simplicity is very difficult to achieve. You must take out the complexity and reduce the statement to something obvious, not hidden behind intellectual phrasing.

A Brand Essence should be familiar in a couple of ways. It should be familiar to the creator (individual or team) in that it should not be a completely new thought – something that has hitherto not been mentioned. This defies the causal process and makes the conclusion (the essence) illogical and, therefore, indefensible. It can and should, however, be born from the concepts, ideas and language completed in the process to date. We can 'leap' to a new place, but we must be able to see where we leapt from.

The Brand Essence should also be familiar to the consumer. Within brand positioning strategy, we are looking to influence the consumer to place our brand in an 'existent reality' (Reis & Trout). The Brand Essence should be congruent with the category, not creating dissonance with their preconceptions. Still, it should clearly align the brand through our assets with a consumer need.

The Brand Essence should be more emotional than rational. We are developing brands in an age where there is only ever a competitive advantage, through product or service innovation, for a limited time due to technological advancement. There are exceptions, usually technology-based, but for most brands, basing a Brand Essence on a physical product or service point of difference is dangerous.

Widgets can be copied, prices matched, service ideas or processes replicated. You can be easily de-positioned by your competitors. What is much more difficult to copy is a Brand Essence based around an emotionally engaging idea. Consider any successful brand. With a little work, you can reduce that brand to a single, simple, emotionally engaging idea.

It is not just for business or competitive reasons that a Brand Essence should be emotionally based. As consumers, as people, we are far from rational. We, at least in the first place, always respond immediately, intuitively, emotionally and non-consciously. A brand, and its essence, should appeal instinctively to the intuitive and emotive consumer; if it 'feels' right, it usually *is* right.

A Brand Essence must be engaging. It must be attractive and credible to the consumer. I would argue that it's impossible, if you follow this process, not to emerge with a concept that is at least relevant to the consumer and your product or service. Often though, the level of engagement depends on the leap we take, ensuring we don't leap so far that the consumer struggles with the relevance.

It terms of the final answer, the best practical advice is to take time for non-conscious creative development - or thinking! The brain is a wonderful thing; even when we have stopped thinking about the answers, it hasn't! If we have run through the Brand Causality Model and been thorough in our conclusions, we will find a solution. If we put ourselves under pressure, the answer will not come. It's worth taking a break when we have finished the Formative Questions and Core Concepts, and again after writing the Brand Story. When we come back to define The Brand Essence, it will emerge from the rigorous investigation and creative inspiration we have invested through the process.

Let's consider our illustrative examples, one last time. As a convergent and causal process, we should present the entire example for each of our airlines.

The sequential nature of the process makes illustration through example difficult. In my experience, it is the smallest 'nuggets' of information that will influence the ultimate brand direction. The forgotten elements of history or the founder's original reasons for creation, the simplest mundane assets that grouped together can tackle a higher end consumer goal or new category insight. Or often an underlying belief identified within the business, which has been an accepted truism, but when focused on can change the direction of the brand and business.

Without accompanying real-life stories, these examples serve two essential purposes: to demonstrate technique and expression – to show the 'causality' in operation, and to illustrate the convergent and sequential nature of the process – how answering one set of questions can lead to answering the next. Regarding expression, I wanted to demonstrate the style and type of language I find most useful. But remember, this is a guide; therefore, we should not feel bound by one style of expression. Instead, use it as a platform to find our own voice and style.

I also wanted to demonstrate how the same tool applied to brands within the same category can produce very different results. Hence the inclusion of the two banks (in our opening) and the two airline examples. In the following example, we can see how the process guides us towards 'the journey' for the national carrier airline, and 'the destination' for our budget airline.

Every brand, new or old, has a wonderfully rich, diverse and specific nature. It is this very nature that makes positioning possible. It would be impossible to recreate the 'lifetime' of four imaginary brands. Hence, within the examples, we can only focus on illustrative and high-order 'example findings' that may well have come from a more detailed examination. We do not recreate the entire process. You should utilise the step-by-step guide to recreate the process when applying it in the real world. Use these examples to understand the nature and expression of the process only.

Bringing It Together 3: The National Carrier Airline

Our Heritage
We played a significant role in the development of aviation in our country, helping connect people locally and nationally and linking our country with the rest of the world.
Our Challenge
A National Airline is no longer the default consumer choice. How do we maintain our volume share in an increasingly competitive market?
The Brand's Business
We are the nation's airline, providing a full-service solution to domestic and international locations.
Consumer Goal
In this category, consumers fly major full-service airlines for the choice, convenience and comfort, but also for the internal self-worth and external status it affords.
Brand Assets
We are part of the nation's history, providing the highest domestic and international standards focused on customer service and care.
The Brand's Truth
A superior customer experience in air travel.
Belief System
We believe in leadership. We believe in the magic of flying. We believe in creating the best experience for our customers every time they fly.
Brand Feeling
Purpose: To continually improve and redefine the expected level of customer service in air travel.

Character: We mirror the service you receive in the best hotels and restaurants: expert and professional, always open, courteous and thoughtful. We pride ourselves on anticipating and catering to all our customers' needs throughout their journey with us.
The Brand's Spirit
Dedicated to making each flight a magical experience.
The Brand Story
We helped establish and evolve the aviation industry in this country to the high standards expected today. We have introduced new aircraft, technology and infrastructure that has seen our brand become recognised throughout our nation and the world as a premium, full-service airline. Our customers' experience is central to our successful development. We provide the highest domestic and international standards in customer service and care. However, we are always looking to improve and redefine this expected level of service. We pride ourselves on anticipating our customers' needs throughout their journey with us, making each and every flight magical.
The Brand Essence
Setting the standard on every journey every time.

Essence unpacked

Removing the country-of-origin characteristics for this generic example removes many points of inspiration! (Think Qantas: The Spirit of Australia). The process leads us to focus on the magical experiences and the journey. The process also pushes us to define the role of a national carrier beyond its heritage (connecting people/nation) that is distinct to them, especially versus budget airlines.

Setting the standard works rationally because it's true – better destinations, airport access, more choice of times and destinations, better seats, service and food and entertainment. But it also appeals to the emotional consumer benefit – the sense of self-worth associated with flying national carriers. A constantly improving and consistent service ethos would result in the airline setting the standard in customer care. It plays against the common complaints of budget services. It will act as a single, clear focus for the development or improvement of product, service and process. This is creatively reflected in Virgin Airlines classic brand line: 'No Ordinary Airline', or the contemporary brand line from Emirates: 'Fly Better'.

It would make staff, customers and frequent flyers proud. Everyone wants to work for the brand setting the standard, and what better reflection than on the sense of self-worth for the customers. When all is said and done, we fly this airline because we get looked after from the closer parking at the main terminal, to the pre-, during and post-flight service. But it needs to be this good every time we fly! A customer service mandate and promise.

Bringing It Together 4: The Budget Airline

Our Heritage
We are a challenger brand, a rebel prepared to take on the establishment in creating and growing a low-fare airline.
Our Challenge
Everyone in our category can be 'budget'. We need to be more to continue to be attractive and survive.
The Brand's Business
We fly regular low-cost flights to a selection of domestic and international destinations.
Consumer Goal
The customers seeking fun, affordable and exciting experiences both domestically and internationally choose us for our reach into new and exotic destinations.
Brand Assets
We are a great value airline, providing a variety of low-cost fares to favourite locations around the world, making air travel more accessible for all.
The Brand's Truth
Helping more people enjoy and experience popular destinations through accessible air travel.
Belief System
We believe in fair; we thrive on change and challenge. We reject tradition and privilege; we are driven by getting the best value price in every aspect of our business, every day.

Brand Feeling
Purpose: To fight hard for discounted air travel, so everyone has access to the freedom and adventure that travel brings.
Character: Youthful, informal, irrepressible and inventive; we were born for adventure.
The Brand's Spirit
Giving adventure and freedom to as many people as we can.
The Brand Story
We fought hard to establish discount air travel into a market dominated by national carriers. We saw the opportunity to fly regular, low-cost flights to selected domestic and international destinations. We brought down the cost of air travel, making it fair, more accessible, helping people enjoy and experience popular destinations. People can now travel to places they have never been or travel more often. We have always challenged tradition. We are a youthful, informal and inventive brand born for adventure! We fight hard to provide low-cost, competitive flights so everyone can experience the sense of adventure and freedom travel brings.
The Brand Essence
Your ticket to discover a different world.

Essence unpacked

A brand should never be positioned on price. Someone will always be cheaper, and they will only erode margin chasing the lowest price. There is always an emotional benefit to the 'cheapness', which provides a better platform for brand growth. Besides, as defined in the challenge, anyone can be budget – we need to define a new role for this brand. The process leads us to the destination, and the ability to explore, experience and discover destinations for the first time or more frequently. We should celebrate the varied experiences that low-cost travel brings, in a way that is a little irreverent and fun but does not over claim.

Ultimately, this discount airline is your ticket to the world by providing low-cost fares. Within the target will be a deep sense (or just an inquisitive nature) to see more of the world (and have some fun) among the safety of peer groups and friends. The brand focus is on the varied destinations and the sense of freedom and excitement travel brings.

REVIEW:

Implications of the Brand Causality Model for Brand Positioning

In has been my intention to supply a practical guide to help position our brand and articulate the detail within the approach to do so successfully. Big questions are dangerous. They should not be answered without thorough consideration and due diligence. The premise of the model is to ask easier, simpler questions that build to the Core Concepts that have the power to define and or transform business.

Now that we've worked through the model together, let's recap the important points in each of the Core and Defining Concepts. There is a natural flow to Brand Causality. The more we summarise, the more familiar and comfortable you will become with the process: 'Repetition is the mother of learning, the father of action, which makes it the architect of accomplishment' (Zig Ziglar).

Key Points when Applying the Model

The Brand's Business

We started through defining what business our brand is in and its speciality or focus: The Brand's Business. Fundamental here is an understanding of the past. In my experience, there is always something to learn from the brand's past, its reason for creation and its development up to now. Find that spark within the brand's heritage and bring it with you on this journey. All too often, I have seen brand strategy, particularly the more 'creative' strategies, establish a direction that does not encompass the historic spirit or current business challenges of the brand. Understanding the past and present business context is a vital part of brand positioning strategy. It cannot be ignored because the consultant or agency has an exciting new direction it is singularly invested in. Ensure the challenges are well defined and, if possible, be selective. Define one key challenge for the business.

I have worked with teams that initially define many challenges but given the time to fully understand each other's challenges, realise they are often one and the same. Defining the Brand's Business should not be easy. If you find yourself stating the obvious, that's fine, but you should make sure you have explored all the potential answers. In this process, we need to embrace the chaos. It can radically alter the fortunes of a business with a bold change in brand direction. Ultimately, define what you want to do and what you are good at (versus the competition).

The Brand's Truth

It is critical in this Core Concept to understand that your potential target is broad, not narrow. You should first understand your category, defined by your articulation of the Brand's Business. You should then seek to explore that category's various motivations, applying the knowledge that consumer motivation exists primarily at a category, not brand, level. You then analyse your brand (and will do so through consumer eyes), articulating your key attributes that add value to the customer. In the final articulation, you define a truth around your brand, based on a core consumer motivation that is empowered by your brand's product and consumer benefits. Answer the very common-sense question: how do we facilitate our chosen customer goal within the category with our product or service? The answer is your Brand's Truth.

I have agonised over many years over descriptors. They are there for a reason! The use of the word 'truth' is meant to encourage a realisation that the world revolves around the category customer, not the product or service. Once a brand identifies its 'reason for being' (its truth) based on helping the consumer reach their goal, everything can change. There is a natural and significant shift in the business; it becomes consumer (not product or service) focused. The benefits of this are as wide as they are far-reaching.

The Brand's Spirit

It is common sense that (awareness being a given) likability is impacted by affiliation. We want to spend time with people we like. We like people because they mirror ourselves in some way physically (gender, age) and share our attitudes and lifestyles (progressive, traditional) and socio-economic groupings. It is, therefore, up to brands to create a positive (sometimes aspirational) perception that reflects and is salient to its audience. All too often, I have found myself playing 'brand personality bingo' with my clients, randomly assigning positive character traits to their brand without considering their customer; hence, the process within the Brand's Spirit.

You need to start with the internal motivation of the brand, the belief system, to ground the answers within the real context of the business. But here you must also be aware of the usual suspects: what are the real cultural beliefs that drive the brand, how do they work together and, when unpacked, what do they really mean? Then you consider the brand feeling, firstly defining the purpose of the brand. Here you need to think big, freeing yourself from increased revenue or market position goals. The key to this question is asking what the brand wants to achieve for the customer, not the business or the shareholders, on a societal and/or a cultural scale. Then, within the context of your business's internal cultural beliefs and driven most by your societal or cultural purpose, you can define the brand's character required to achieve those aims. The character of the brand is, of course, vital, but rather than randomly assigning positive traits you now have a brief to follow and to inspire.

The Brand Story

The art of storytelling is difficult, even agonising. However, this model guides you into it through using your findings from the previous Core Concepts to inspire a story about our brand. This is best done in isolation, rather than the workshop context. And keep to the 100 words. Sacrifice is the key to simplicity, and no more so than here.

I always enjoy and fear this part of the process! My personal advice is to just put pen to paper – and not only figuratively. I will often get some 'real' paper and dust off my pen for this section (something happens when you remove yourself from a screen!). Here, language becomes essential, not just the ability to be concise but more importantly, the ability to inspire. But you can do this. No one is better placed, having been through this process, to write your Brand Story. Lastly, stay aware that the Brand Essence may emerge from this process (not forced). In trying to summarise the Core Concepts, and while being concise and inspirational, the answer quite often appears. If it does, make sure to write it down!

The Brand Essence

In the ultimate confluence of the process, something naturally emerges or is sometimes hard-earned. A good test for the Brand Essence is that it must be true to the product or service, engaging to the consumer and distinct from the competition. If it passes those tests, you are well on your way to the answer.

When I have a few potential answers, I like to spend some time thinking about the application to the brand. How might each one of the possible Brand Essences impact the brand and the business? What are the practical implications of the different directions? Does one inspire a clearer direction in terms of implementation and execution? When I present the Brand Essence to a client, it is usually followed by a 'why this works' chart, referencing why it is true to the product, engaging to the customer and distinct from the competition. This chart is followed by a 'implications for business' chart, detailing the potential impact of the strategy on the practical running of the business. This chart is the easiest to write by utilising the best 'essence'. Hence, (typically) if the new Brand Essence inspires little positive change or clear recommendations within the business, it is weaker than one that does.

An Initial Evolutionary Process

Brand positioning is not easy. It involves intense, high-order bursts of concentration. It requires different skills at different stages of the process. Sometimes analytic and thorough and occasionally creative and convergent, the rewards are always great.

Like life, the process can sometimes be best understood backwards. I will often revisit sections and findings, changing and evolving answers. In its initial creation, there is a need to be flexible, allowing the time and freedom for non-conscious processing. By letting the ideas formulate and evolve, we will get there! However, once decided, we must be resolute. Good brand positioning will become the reference point for everything in a business and, unless the business changes significantly, should be so for many years.

Always keep in mind that this is a guide. Use the model for individual purposes. Once you have learnt and understood the process, you can change it, make it better, and tailor it to your personal or commercial needs.

It has been my intention to provide an instructive, practical process or framework to position a brand in the market and mind of the consumer. For those that do not have a brand to immediately apply these new skills to, we can run the exercise on our personal brand (ourselves as individuals). Everyone has access and enough knowledge to be able to complete this exercise. The more the process is used, the easier it will become.

The Importance of Brand Positioning

The Brand Causality Model not only requires detailed knowledge of the brand but enforces the disciplines of brevity and clarity to arrive at focused single-minded ideas. The aim is to clearly and definitively position your brand in the marketplace and guide the consumer to create a positive and engaging brand perception. Convergent thinking simplifies brand meaning and definition to just a few words and a single concept. I cannot overstate the power of simplicity within brand positioning and the subsequent case of application and execution that follows.

Brand, business and product failures are countless, and most markets are mature, competitive and increasingly fragmented. Despite our psychological and behavioural complexities, I believe we all yearn for simple guidance, for clarity of understanding and direction.

The process articulated here is formulated with this presumption. It makes the 'what happens next' easier. Going through the process always results in a collective sigh of relief ('We know who we are!') and a renewed energy and enthusiasm for the brand ('We know where we are going!'). After workshops in my consultancy, clients will report the benefit of shared understanding and the energy that it creates. It should not be underestimated, which is why I would urge that this process is completed within a team (if possible). Collective input and shared understanding of the resultant brand direction within an organisation has an exponential impact on the brand or business in question. Imagine product development, design, sales, marketing and customer care teams all aligned and empowered with the same brand direction!

A clear brand direction makes the everyday running of a business easier. The team should now understand what works (and what doesn't). New product development becomes more focused, sales teams understand value beyond discounting, marketing becomes less scattergun – doing fewer things better, and customer care knows how the brand should respond. There are great cost-efficiencies in shared understanding and direction.

All of this is achievable by asking straightforward questions, from which the Core Concepts emerge to form a Brand Story and Essence that are the foundations of our brand now and into the future. I am often asked about the benefits of brand positioning. I would counter, can an organisation afford to *not* clearly define and direct their brand?

Where to from here for you and your brand? The 'what happens next' question is dependent on several factors, but it is primarily based on your findings from the Brand Causality process and how different they are to the current brand positioning. As always, the need for dramatic or wholesale change is rare. Positioning your brand through this process is about establishing a blueprint for everyone who comes into contact with it. It is about codifying your brand to make business decisions more consistent and manageable. Typically, over time, the brand positioning pervades every aspect of your business because those in key positions have a 'true north' to follow.

I have often compared brands to people in this book. Again, when we come to a realisation about ourselves, be it a willingness to change, to develop or try something different, it will take time for learnt attitudes to impact our behaviour (you don't wake up a different person). The same is true of applying the brand strategy to our brand and business. We may want to change our products or service, our brand identity, or we may want to develop new communications through new channels. My advice is to slowly evolve the brand in line with the new strategy over time. The point is, you now have a guide to do so. It doesn't have to all happen overnight (but it should happen!).

I wish you all the very best of luck in your brand journey.

Made in the USA
Monee, IL
04 November 2026

67381746R10075